macramé
AT HOME

ADD BOHO-CHIC CHARM TO EVERY ROOM WITH 20 PROJECTS
FOR STUNNING PLANT HANGERS, WALL ART, PILLOWS AND MORE

natalie ranae
MACRAMÉ ARTIST AND INSTRUCTOR

PAGE STREET
PUBLISHING CO.

PAGE STREET
PUBLISHING CO.

First published in 2018 by
Page Street Publishing Co.
27 Congress Street, Suite 105
Salem, MA 01970
www.pagestreetpublishing.com

Distributed by Macmillan, sales in Canada by The Canadian Manda Group.

21 20 19   4 5

ISBN-13: 978-1-62414-528-5
ISBN-10: 1-62414-528-0

Library of Congress Control Number: 2017957939

Cover and book design by Page Street Publishing Co.
Photography by Jennifer Cornthwaite of Jennifer See Studios

Printed and bound in the United States.

dedication

To every creative and artistic soul seeking to learn more.
And to my incredible husband and best friend, Shawn.

contents

introduction

Macramé is back! Like most things in life, everything comes back around in style eventually, and macramé is finally having its moment again. Except this time around it's characterized by a new modern look, much less brown and orange jute, and fewer owl patterns that characterized the 1970s. Macramé, which at its simplest is the art of creating patterns out of knots, has made a huge emergence into modern home decor, whether that's through artistic wall hangings, beautiful and practical plant hangers or by being worked into everyday objects, home accents or furniture. If you're looking to add some unique textural designs to your home while also learning a fun new craft, you've picked up the right book!

My first introduction to the world of macramé was a trio of macramé owls that my grandmother had hung up in the hallway in her cottage. One had a pair of large, red wood beads for eyes, and I remember my younger sister and me being so afraid of them that my mom had to hide them when we would visit! This book is evidence that a lot has changed since those days, as I am now completely obsessed with this wonderful art form. I'm so happy and fortunate to spend my days designing new macramé pieces, making large-scale custom orders and spreading the love of macramé though workshops and tutorials.

I love macramé because it offers the opportunity for endless creativity. The combination of knots and patterns allows you to take a piece in so many different directions. I've been a maker my entire life, doing everything from knitting and crocheting at a young age to becoming a professional jeweler and metalsmith, and I can honestly say that macramé is one of my favorite outlets for creativity. However, consider this fair warning that macramé is extremely addicting! After learning even just a few of the knots and projects in this book, your brain will be filled with an endless amount of ideas, and before you know it your home will be filled with macramé, like mine is!

Whether this is your first time encountering macramé or you've had some experience with the medium, you'll find projects in this book for you. I divided the projects into three categories—beginner, intermediate and advanced. If you're new to macramé, I'd advise you to hold off on attempting the advanced projects until you're able to work through some of the beginner and intermediate projects at a good pace. Each project has a unique "variation" that I designed to change the look of the design. All of the projects are organized into three chapters: Wall Hangings (page 49), Plant Hangers (page 93) and Home Accents (page 117). Feel free to start in whichever chapter you're most excited about and bounce around projects from there. There's no "right" way to use this book, but my hope for you is that it will push you to continue to express yourself creatively, seek inspiration and challenge yourself!

getting started

WHAT YOU NEED TO KNOW

Macramé, like any craft, takes patience and attention to detail. However, it's relatively easy to pick up, and highly addicting once you understand the basics!

You don't need any fancy tools or apparatus to make macramé on; you simply need to be able to hang your project from something. You can get creative and string your piece from something like a curtain rod or hooks on the back of a door. I prefer to work on a clothing rack that rolls because I can move it around easily and its height is adjustable for when I start working lower on a piece. Using large S-hooks, I hang all my projects from the rack and it's the perfect way to work. I like this setup because it's more ergonomically suited for your body, which is important if you're spending a substantial amount of time on a project!

Besides rope, what you'll need for each project is a good pair of scissors or shears, as they will make your life much easier. In all the projects, I work with 100 percent natural cotton cord. You can use either three-strand or braided cord for most projects, but I also list which I use in each project. Using three-strand or braided slightly changes the look and texture of each project, but they are largely interchangeable. Another helpful tip is to wrap a little bit of masking tape on the ends of your cords before you start. That helps prevent the cords from unraveling while you're working with them. Once a cord unravels you can't put it back together and you don't want it to interrupt where you are tying knots.

Each project will have a more in-depth look at tools needed, rope type and length requirements. There's also a resource guide I put together for you at the back of the book (page 167) because macramé supplies can sometimes be hard to find!

I hope you're excited to learn and ready to make some projects with me!

useful terms & phrases

Working Cords: When tying a knot, these are the cords you are handling and physically using to tie the knot. For example, the working cords are the two cords on the outside of four cords used to tie a square knot (see page 14).

Filler Cords: These are the cords that knots are being tied around. They are typically the cords in the middle of the knots. For example, the two filler cords are in the middle of a square knot (see page 14).

"Tight to the row/knots before": This phrase refers to the space left between each row or knot and is indicating for you to leave no space. This means the knots row after row are tied with no space in between each knot and row.

"Ending with a point or sharp point": This is normally indicating to end with one type of knot, usually a double half hitch. Learn how to tie it with a point on page 37.

Fringe: The frayed unraveled rope usually at the bottom of the piece.

Unravel: This refers to undoing a piece of rope. See my method for unraveling rope on page 43.

knots & patterns

This section will teach you how to make all the knots and patterns used in this book. Be sure to tie your knots with the same strength and tightness to keep your pattern looking consistent. This will help make your work look neat. Remember, these are knots, so tie them firmly so that they don't come loose, especially in your last row before your fringe. Try practicing these knots before working on the projects if you feel it will help. Alternatively, before you start a certain project, take a look at the list of knots used and reference this section to practice beforehand.

Most patterns can be made in an increasing and decreasing pattern. Similar to knitting and crochet, decreasing patterns typically use 2 fewer knots on each row consecutively until you reach your desired amount. To increase a pattern you add 2 knots evenly to each row until your reach your desired amount. Each project will clearly show you step by step how to increase or decrease for that pattern.

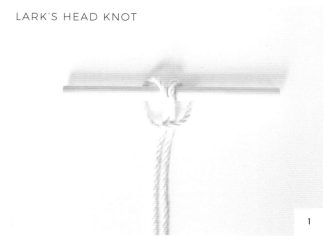

1

2

REVERSE LARK'S HEAD KNOT

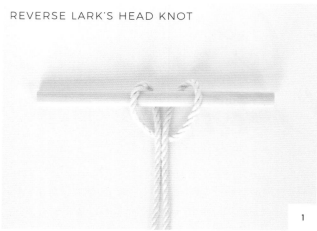

1

2

LARK'S HEAD KNOT

Commonly used to attach your rope to another piece of rope, dowel or ring.

1. Begin by folding your cord in half. Place the loop over the mounting cord or dowel, carry the loop around back and bring the two ends through the loop.

2. Pull tight.

REVERSE LARK'S HEAD KNOT

1. Fold the cord in half. Place the loop under the mounting cord or dowel, carry the loop around to the front and bring the two ends through the loop.

2. Pull tight.

HALF KNOT

This simple knot is used to create a square knot; it is rarely used on its own because it can come undone easily.

LEFT FACING

1. Begin the half knot by bringing cord 1 over the fillers (cords 2 and 3) and under cord 4. Cord 4 goes under the fillers and up through cords 1 and 2. Pull tight.

RIGHT FACING

1. Begin the half knot by bringing cord 4 over the fillers (cords 2 and 3) and under cord 1. Cord 1 goes under the fillers and up through cords 4 and 3.

2. Pull tight.

LEFT-FACING HALF KNOT

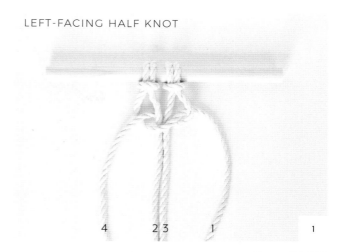

RIGHT-FACING HALF KNOT

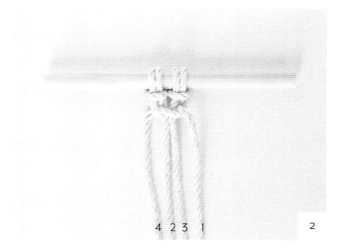

LEFT-FACING SQUARE KNOT

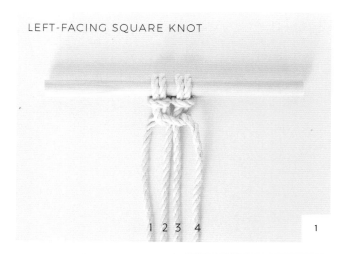

1 2 3 4   1

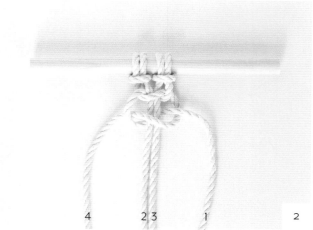

4   2 3   1   2

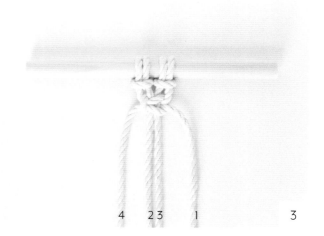

4   2 3   1   3

SQUARE KNOT

This is one of the most versatile and commonly used knots in macramé. I always tie left-facing square knots throughout a piece to keep it consistent, though you can also tie all right-facing knots (see next page).

LEFT FACING

1. Refer to left-facing half knot (page 13).

2. Place cord 4 over fillers and under cord 1. Cord 1 goes under fillers and up through cords 3 and 4.

3. Pull tight.

RIGHT FACING

You can also tie all right-facing square knots throughout your work, but choose either the left- or right-facing variation to keep your work consistent.

1. Refer to right-facing half knot (page 13).

2. Place cord 1 over fillers and under cord 4. Cord 4 goes under fillers and up through cords 1 and 2.

3. Pull tight.

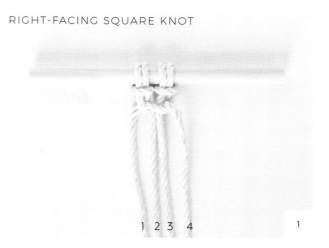

1 2 3 4

1

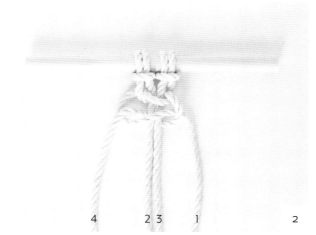

4 2 3 1

2

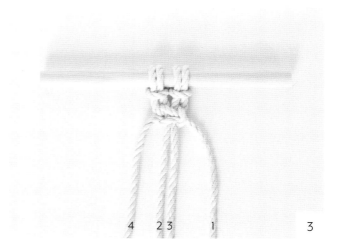

4 2 3 1

3

SQUARE KNOT WITH MULTIPLE FILLER CORDS

1

SQUARE KNOT WITH MULTIPLE FILLER CORDS
AND MULTIPLE WORKING CORDS

1

SQUARE KNOT WITH MULTIPLE FILLER CORDS

Changing the amount of cords you tie a knot with, or around, greatly impacts the overall look of the knot. This makes a great accent knot that you can incorporate into your work.

1. Repeat all of the steps from either the left-facing or the right-facing square knot, but increase the amount of filler cords to more than the regular amount of 2 cords. Pull relatively tight, but making sure the cords don't overlap. Situate them so that they lie flat, side by side next to each other.

SQUARE KNOT WITH MULTIPLE FILLER CORDS
AND MULTIPLE WORKING CORDS

This also makes a great accent knot to use in your work.

1. Repeat all of the steps from either the left-facing or the right-facing square knot, but increase the amount of working cords from the usual one on each side and increase the filler cords to more than the regular amount of 2 cords. Pull relatively tight, making sure the cords don't overlap but instead lie flat, side by side next to each other.

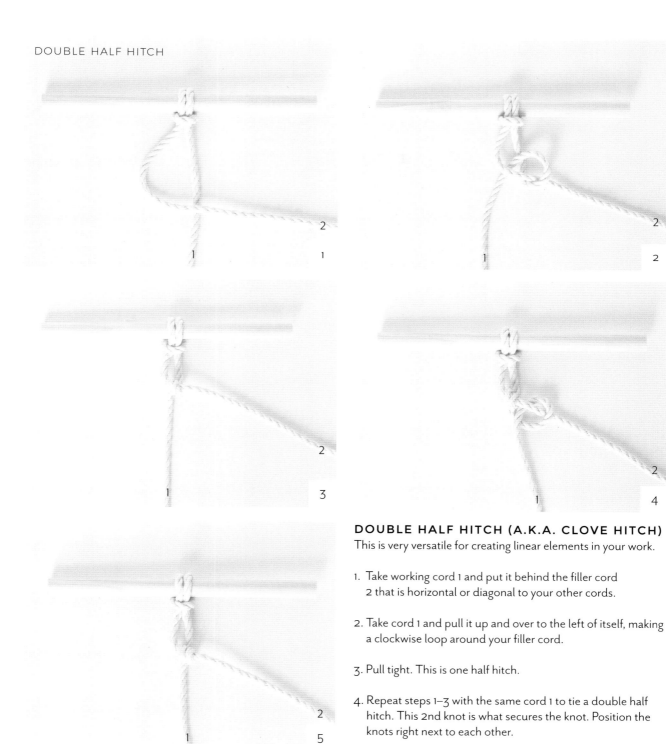

DOUBLE HALF HITCH (A.K.A. CLOVE HITCH)

This is very versatile for creating linear elements in your work.

1. Take working cord 1 and put it behind the filler cord 2 that is horizontal or diagonal to your other cords.

2. Take cord 1 and pull it up and over to the left of itself, making a clockwise loop around your filler cord.

3. Pull tight. This is one half hitch.

4. Repeat steps 1–3 with the same cord 1 to tie a double half hitch. This 2nd knot is what secures the knot. Position the knots right next to each other.

5. Pull tight.

OVERHAND KNOT

1

2

REEF KNOT

OVERHAND KNOT

This knot can be tied with multiple cords or a single cord.

1. Pass the end of the cord around itself and through the loop it forms.

2. Pull tight.

REEF KNOT (A.K.A. SQUARE KNOT)

This is one of the most common knots; you use it to tie your shoes! Not to be confused with the other square knot.

1. Using 2 cords, take cord 1 and cross it over cord 2, and then under and over cord 2.

2. Cross cord 1 over and under cord 2, then up and through the loop created by cord 2.

3. Pull tight.

1

GATHERING KNOT (A.K.A. WRAPPING KNOT)

This knot is typically used to finish a plant hanger by gathering the cords together.

1. Fold a long working cord and lay it against the filler cords, leaving a 3-inch (7.5-cm) or longer tail on the bottom. The tail length changes depending on the length of gathering knot you are tying.

2. Wrap the cord upwards, forming a small nub at the bottom. Holding the wrapped cord in place, continue wrapping the long end around the gathered cords and short tail. In the photo, the short tail sticks out on the left (the end is taped), and the little nub is on the right. Continue wrapping toward the loop, until you reach your desired wrapped length.

3. Pass the end through the loop.

(continued)

2

3

← pull here

4

5

6

4. Pull the loop tight by pulling the end of the cord on the bottom.

5. Trim the top cord short enough that it will hide in the gathering knot. Pull the bottom end of the cord again, so the short piece you just trimmed is pulled through the bundle and is hidden. Be careful not to pull so hard that your knot comes apart.

6. Trim the other end close to the wrapped cords, hiding it.

GATHERING KNOT FOR A TASSEL

When I tie a gathering knot for a tassel, I leave a longer tail on the cord I am pulling on in step 4 and then I unravel the longer tail so it becomes part of the fringe. You do not have to do it this way, but it is why some of the cords for gathering knots throughout the book are longer.

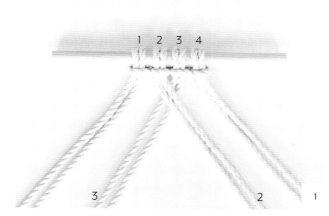

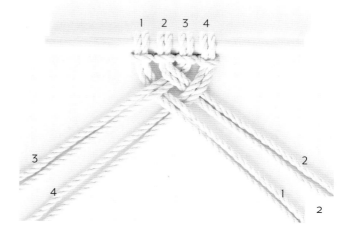

WEAVE KNOT

This knot can be done with one or more cords to change the look of the knot. This example is done with a grouping of 2 cords and a total of 8 cords.

1. Cross grouping 2 over 3.

2. Cross grouping 1 under 3, and cross grouping 4 over 2. Then cross grouping 1 over 4.

3. Cross 4 over 3, and then 2 over 1.

4. Cross 3 over 2, and continue the pattern to secure the ropes in place.

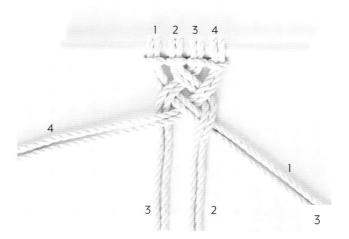

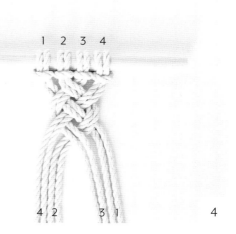

1

SQUARE KNOT SINNET

This sinnet is used a lot in classic plant hangers and in wall hanging designs.

1. Begin tying square knots (instructions on page 14).

2. Continue until you reach your desired length. Each individual square knot you tie consecutively increases the overall length of the sinnet. Be sure to tie each knot tight to each other, leaving minimal gaps so you don't see much of the filler cords. You can slightly push up on the knots if you are finding there are gaps in between. Do not tie 2 left-facing or right-facing half knots back to back because your piece will begin to twist (see Half Knot Sinnet, page 24).

2

SQUARE KNOT SINNET WITH DIFFERENT WORKING CORDS (PINE TREE PATTERN)

1. When creating a pine tree pattern, you are continually using new working cords from a series of knots usually above where you are tying the pine tree sinnet. See photos for further clarification on which ropes to use. The new working cords you use are usually above and diagonal to where you are looking to tie the pine tree sinnet. To get the full effect of this pattern, continue this pattern, alternating the sinnet placement on each row.

2. Tie square knots (page 14) as usual on the same filler cords, but use different working cords for each square knot. Place the working cord behind or out of the way after tying each knot.

3. Continue to your desired length.

PINE TREE PATTERN

1

2

3

HALF KNOT SINNET

HALF KNOT SINNET

1. Refer to the half knot instructions (page 13) and repeatedly tie the same left-facing half knots to your desired length. This creates a right-twisting sinnet.

2. Be sure to tie each knot tight to each other, leaving minimal gaps so you don't see much of the filler cords. You can slightly push up on the knots if you are finding there are gaps in between.

Tie a left-twisting sinnet by tying only right-facing half knots.

DOUBLE HALF KNOT SINNET

I use this sinnet in the Luma Rope Light project on page 123.

1. Use 6 cords—2 filler cords and 2 working cords on one side of the filler cords and 2 on the other. Tie a left-facing half knot (page 13) with the inner working cords, around the filler cords.

2. Move the inner working cords out of the way and tie a left-facing half knot with the outer working cords, around the filler cords.

3. Repeat steps 1 and 2 until you reach your desired length. By tying all left-facing half knots, the sinnet will twist to the right. If you want your sinnet to twist to the left, tie all right-facing half knots instead.

DOUBLE HALF KNOT SINNET

1

2

3

ALTERNATING SQUARE KNOT

1

2

3

VARIED SPACING

1

ALTERNATING SQUARE KNOT

This is one of the most common and simple patterns in macramé. It can be tied with or without space between each row. This changes the look of the pattern completely! Try experimenting with different spacing to vary the look.

1. For the 1st row, tie a square knot (page 14) with every 4 cords.

2. Excluding the first 2 and last 2 cords in the 2nd row, tie a square knot with every 4 cords.

3. Repeat steps 1 and 2 until you reach your desired length.

VARIED SPACING

Here is an example of how different the same pattern looks by changing the space between the rows.

1. Repeat steps 1–3, leaving a consistent space in between each row.

DECREASING ALTERNATING SQUARE KNOT

1

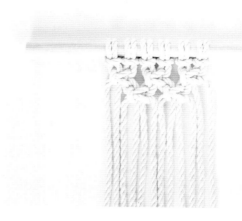

2

DECREASING ALTERNATING SQUARE KNOT (FULL AND OPEN)

1. For the 1st row, tie a full row of square knots (page 14) with every 4 cords.

2. Excluding the first 2 and last 2 cords in the 2nd row, tie a square knot with every 4 cords.

3. Exclude the first 4 and last 4 cords in the 3rd row.

Continue this same pattern with more cords to make a decreasing pattern larger.

4. To create the open version, tie square knots only on the outer ends of row 1.

3

4

INCREASING ALTERNATING SQUARE KNOT

1

2

3

INCREASING ALTERNATING SQUARE KNOT (FULL AND OPEN)

1. For the 1st row, tie a square knot (page 14) using the 4 cords in the middle.

2. Skipping the first 2 and last 2 cords in the 2nd row, tie a square knot with every 4 cords.

3. Tie 1 full row of square knots across all of the cords.

Continue the pattern with more cords to make the increasing pattern larger.

4. To create the open version, simply skip the middle square knot in row 3, only tying square knots on the outer ends.

4

ALTERNATING SQUARE KNOT SINNET

Tip: You can tie an alternating pattern with many different knots and sinnets! To get more variety in your square knot sinnet patterns, try changing the amount of knots you use in each row. For example try tying 1 square knot in one row, and in the next tie 3 square knots and repeat that pattern.

1. For the 1st row, tie a square knot sinnet (page 22) 2 square knots long with every 4 cords.

2. Excluding the first 2 and last 2 cords in the 2nd row, tie a square knot sinnet 2 square knots long with every 4 cords.

3. Repeat steps 1 and 2 until you reach the desired length.

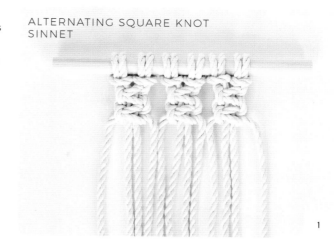

1

2

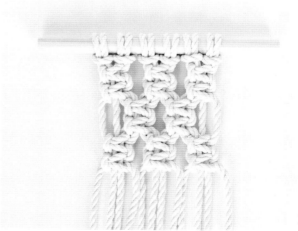

3

4 SQUARE KNOT CLUSTER

1

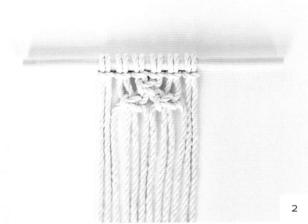

2

3

4 SQUARE KNOT CLUSTER (ALTERNATING SQUARE KNOTS)

This cluster can be done anywhere with a minimum of 8 cords; leave consistent space in between each row or tie them tight together. I like to use them as small accent knots within a project.

1. In the middle of the 8 cords, tie 1 square knot (page 14).

2. Tie 2 increasing alternating square knots (page 28) in the 2nd row.

3. Tie 1 last square knot in the middle of the 8 cords.

SQUARE KNOT OPEN DIAMOND

SQUARE KNOT OPEN DIAMOND

1. For the 1st row, starting with the 4 cords in the middle, tie 1 square knot (page 14).

2. Continue tying 1 row of increasing alternating square knots (page 28), stepping down diagonally every 2 cords, until you reach your desired width or the edge on either side.

3. Continue tying 1 row of decreasing alternating square knots (page 27), stepping inward every 2 cords, until you reach the center of the diamond on each side.

4. Finish by tying 1 square knot in the middle of the cords.

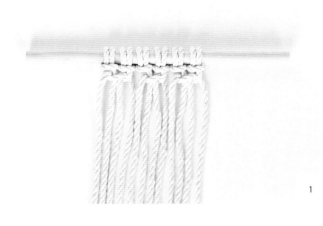

1

2

3

ALTERNATING HALF KNOT

Approach this the exact same way you would tie the alternating square knot (page 26) for increasing, decreasing and so on. Make sure you tie either left- or right-facing half knots consistently throughout the pattern.

1. For the 1st row, tie a half knot (page 13) with every 4 cords.

2. Excluding the first 2 and last 2 cords in the 2nd row, tie a half knot with every 4 cords.

3. Repeat steps 1 and 2 until your desired length.

CONTINUOUS LARK'S HEAD KNOT

This can be done vertically and horizontally.

1. Using the working cord, wrap it in front of the filler cord and then back around the filler cord and around and on top of itself.

2. Wrap the working cord behind and then bring it forward around the filler cord, then pass it through the loop created by the working cord.

3. Pull tight and continue as many times as desired.

1

CONTINUOUS LARK'S HEAD KNOT
(CONTINUED)

2

3

CONTINUOUS REVERSE LARK'S HEAD KNOT

1

2

CONTINUOUS REVERSE LARK'S HEAD KNOT
This can also be done vertically and horizontally. I incorporated this horizontally into a few projects in the book.

1. Using the working cord, wrap it behind the filler cord and then back around the filler cord and behind itself.

2. Wrap the working cord in front and then bring it behind and around the filler cord, then pass it through the loop created by the working cord.

3. Pull tight and continue as many times as desired.

3

DIAGONAL DOUBLE HALF HITCH

1

2

HORIZONTAL/DIAGONAL DOUBLE HALF HITCH (CLOVE HITCH)

Tip: When tying multiple rows of horizontal or diagonal double half hitches and you want them tight to each other with no space in between rows, do the following. After pulling the working cord around the filler cord, pull the cord away from you with some force (backward away from the piece); as you do this, you should see the knot move closer to the row above.

1. Hold your filler cord horizontally or diagonally at the angle you want it to be.

2. Tie double half hitches (page 17) continuously along the filler cord.

REVERSE DOUBLE HALF HITCH

1. The back of double half hitches are just as beautiful and textured as the front. The simplest way to tie reverse double half hitches is to simply flip your piece around and tie a regular double half hitch in the desired spot. Then flip your work back around to continue your pattern.

REVERSE DOUBLE HALF HITCH

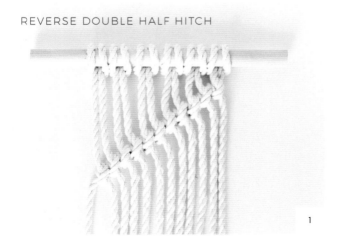

1

TYING AROUND A RING OR DOWEL

1. When tying double half hitches (page 17) around a ring or dowel, treat the ring or dowel as the filler cord and begin tying double half hitches around it starting from one side.

2. Continue tying double half hitches until you get to the end.

TYING AROUND A RING OR DOWEL

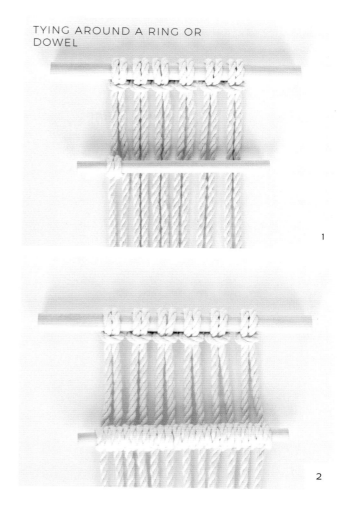

1

2

VERTICAL DOUBLE HALF HITCH

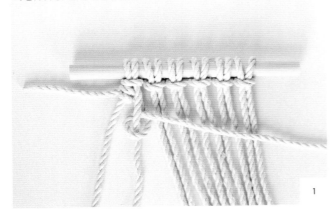

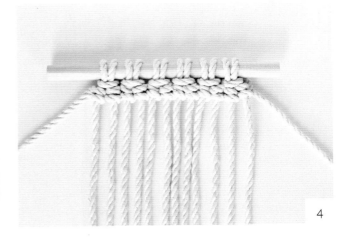

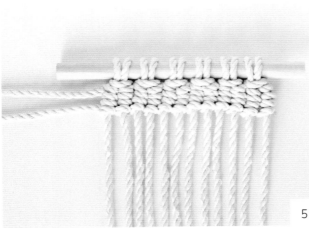

VERTICAL DOUBLE HALF HITCH

1. When tying a vertical double half hitch, the cords hanging vertically are your filler cords. With a separate cord, attach the working cord to the first filler cord by tying a half hitch (page 17).

2. Make a double half hitch by tying a second half hitch on the same cord.

3. Pull tight to finish your double half hitch.

4. Wrap the working cord around the next adjacent filler cord, and tie 1 double half hitch. Continue tying vertical double half hitches working left to right, tying one double half hitch on each filler cord.

5. Once you are at the end, begin working right to left beneath the row above.

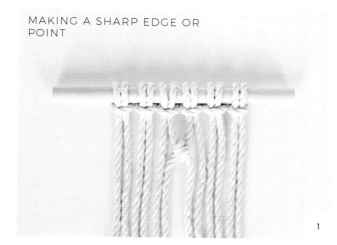

1

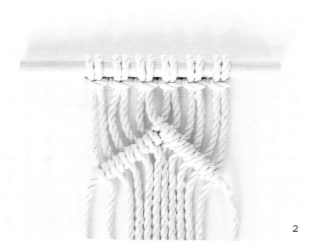

2

MAKING A SHARP EDGE OR POINT WITH DOUBLE HALF HITCHES

When tying double half hitches (page 17), sometimes you want your work to have a sharp edge or point to complete a diamond or V shape. This is how I tied the majority of my diamonds throughout the book.

WORKING FROM THE TOP

1. Start with the top of the diamond. With 2 cords, make one cord the working cord and tie it around the other cord using a double half hitch.

2. Now continue tying diagonal double half hitches (page 34) around both of the cords from step 1. The first knot makes the point.

FINISHING THE BOTTOM

3. To finish the bottom of a diamond, tie diagonal double half hitches until you reach just the two filler cords in the middle.

4. Take the filler cord from one of the rows of double half hitches, make it the working cord and tie a double half hitch around the other filler cord tightly, leaving no space between the knots. This creates the point at the bottom, just like the top of the diamond.

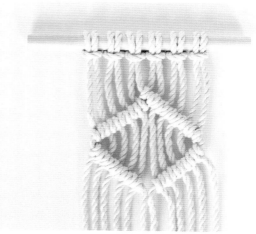

3

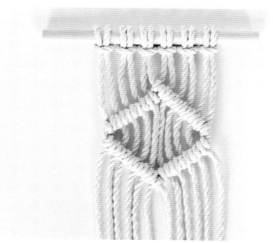

4

DIAMONDS

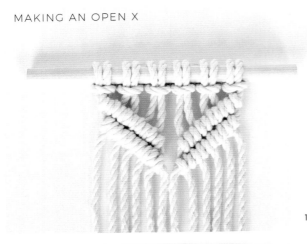

1

MAKING AN OPEN X

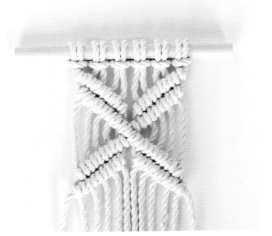

1

2

DIAMONDS

You can tie a series of diagonal double half hitches (page 34) to form a diamond. You can do this in two ways: by creating sharp corners halfway through the diamond or by making a slightly softer look on the corners.

1. To create sharp corners, shown on the left side in the photo, follow the same steps from "Making a Sharp Edge or Point with Double Half Hitches" (page 37) at the sides of the diamond.

   For softer-looking corners, shown on the right side, continue using the same filler cord but just change the angle you hold the filler cord and continue tying diagonal double half hitches.

MAKING AN OPEN X

1. Tie a series of diagonal double half hitches (page 34) angling in toward each other.

2. Once you reach the middle, tie one double half hitch following "Making a Sharp Edge or Point with Double Half Hitches" (page 37) to join the center only. Then continue to tie diagonal double half hitches angling out from the center.

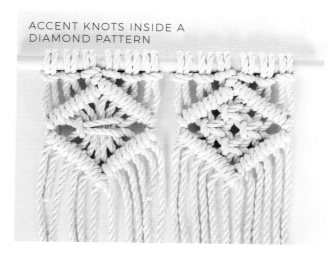

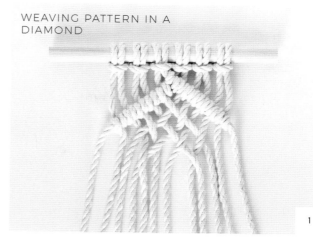

ACCENT KNOTS INSIDE A DIAMOND PATTERN

While tying a diamond from double half hitches or square knots, you can add different accent knots in the center of the diamond. The left is a square knot with multiple filler cords (page 16) and the right is a square knot cluster (page 30).

WEAVING PATTERN IN A DIAMOND

1. Using the cords within the upper half of the diamond, take each and weave it over and under the rope beside it.

2. Continue this with all the cords in the middle of the diamond. When you get to the middle of the diamond, gradually taper in toward the lower part of the diamond.

3. Use the two end working cords as the filler cords, hold on a diagonal and finish the diamond using one of the methods from "Diamonds" on the previous page.

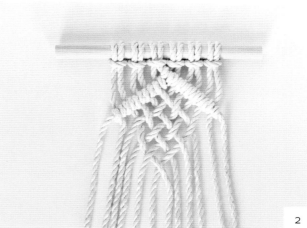

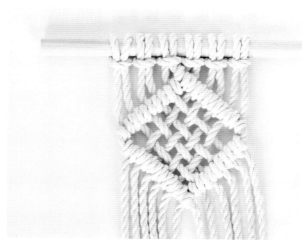

Tips & Tricks

This section outlines some general tips, tricks and advice you should know when starting macramé.

I use mostly three-strand natural cotton rope throughout this book. If you're excited to make almost every project in this book, buying 2 mm, 3 mm and 5 mm sizes in bulk could be helpful!

GETTING SET UP

I like to hang my work from a clothes rack using S-hooks and let the gravity and tension from the weight of the rope hold the work down. Because you use so much rope when making macramé, I like to make cutting the rope as easy and convenient as possible. I use a plastic milk crate and insert a wooden dowel through the center of the spool of rope and the crate to make pulling and cutting the rope easier. Before cutting each strand of rope, wrap a small strip of masking tape around the section you want to cut, and then cut through the middle of the tape. This will keep your rope from unraveling while you work. Yes, you end up unraveling some of the rope to make a fringe, but without tape, you can't control how much it unravels and you don't want it to unravel in sections where you still need to tie knots. That would make your work look messy and uneven.

USE CONSISTENT TENSION

Pay attention to how tight you pull and tighten your cords, as it affects the size of your knots and the overall consistency of your piece. Keep your knots consistent by using the same amount of tension on each knot. This gets easier with practice.

FIXING MISTAKES

The great thing about macramé is that it is easy enough to undo any knot you tie, and if you make a mistake, it's not irreversible. If you find that you've made a mistake far back in your work, you can do one of two things. You can simply leave it and learn for next time, because most likely you will be the only one who notices it. Or if you're like me, and it's going to drive you crazy, you can undo it. Unfortunately, you will have to undo all the knots that were made after the mistake and then continue the pattern from that point. To avoid this, keep checking your work as you go.

BUNDLING CORDS

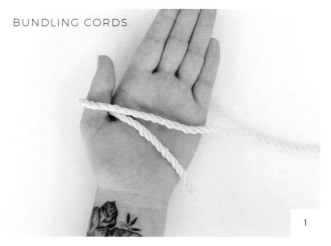

1

2

3

BUNDLING CORDS

When you're working with cords that are extremely long, bundle them to make things easier. This helps keep your cords from getting knotted or tangled when you're working. It also makes working more efficient because you don't have to pull so many feet of rope through each knot. You can bundle the ropes in whatever way is easiest for you or use this method to keep the bundle from getting tangled.

1. Hold one end in your palm and tie a figure eight around your thumb and pinky finger until you reach the end.

2. Wrap the end of the cord around itself at least three times and tuck the end into itself.

3. Pull tight.

MY METHOD FOR UNRAVELING ROPE   1

2

MY METHOD FOR UNRAVELING ROPE

To get the look I like in my macramé pieces, I usually follow two steps when I am working with three-strand cotton rope.

1. Unravel the cords to your desired length/height. The cords will be very "kinky" after.

2. To make the fringe more full and frayed looking, I unravel each of the three strands of rope by twisting it in the opposite direction the cords are naturally twisting, while holding the top with one hand. Then I carefully run my fingers through it until I reach the ends and carefully let go of the top, then the bottom.

3. Do these steps for all of the fringe for a nice full look. I have also found this to be the smoothest technique.

USING A COMB

1. If I have a relatively short fringe on a piece and I want it very unraveled, I use a wide-tooth comb and carefully comb through it after I've unraveled the three-strand rope. Make sure not to comb through it too aggressively, or you risk breaking the small fibers of rope that make up the strands.

3

USING A COMB   1

USING A FORK 1

USING A FORK

1. You can also use a fork to brush out the very bottom of the fringe. After unraveling the rope into its three "kinky" strands, use a fork held at a 45-degree angle to carefully brush through the bottom of the fringe. Don't use this technique any higher than 4 inches (10 cm) up from the base of the fringe, as it will end up making a mess of the small strands and knot up the ends.

UNEVEN ENDS

1. If you're at the end of your piece and your ropes aren't quite the same length, you can unravel your pieces using "My Method for Unraveling Rope" (page 43).

2. The uneven ends will blend together, and the different heights will be less obvious.

UNEVEN ENDS 1

KNOWING HOW MUCH ROPE TO USE FOR YOUR OWN PROJECT

There is no easy answer or perfect formula for figuring out how much rope to use. The amount of rope you need varies based on the complexity and density of your design. The pattern, tension, arrangement and open space all affect how much rope your project needs. Again, this is something that is very hard to figure out, and usually gets much easier the more you practice macramé. The best tip I can give is that as you make new pieces, compare the amount of cord you used for the project, and then make an educated guess based on the projects you've made. I usually note how much cord I used for a piece and the length I cut each strand of rope, and this helps me if I make it again or need to compare the lengths for future projects. When in doubt, leave yourself a little more rope when you're beginning. If you are really unsure, you can always test the rope length you need by making a sample piece. Overall, this is something that comes with time and practice.

IF YOU RUN OUT OF CORD WHEN WORKING ON A PROJECT

If you happen to run out of cord while working, there are a few ways to add more cord. Whichever method you use, make sure you leave a long tail on both ends so that you can use a large-eye needle to sew the ends into the back of your work. When in doubt, weave the new cord into the back of the previous knot, and continue knotting with the new cord.

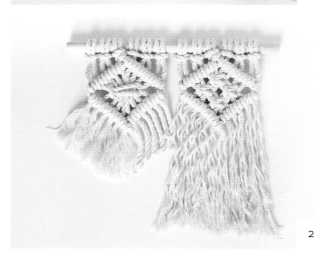

2

ADDING A CORD BY TYING A SQUARE KNOT

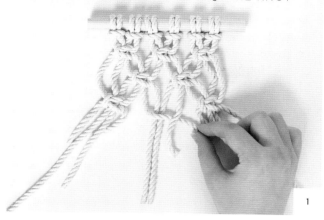

1

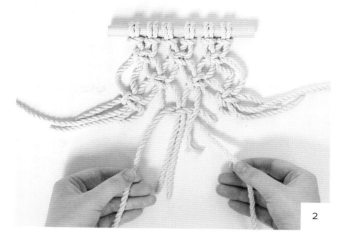

2

3

4

ADDING A CORD BY TYING A SQUARE KNOT

1. Start a square knot (page 14) as usual.

2. Fold the new working cord in half and loop it around the filler cords from the back of the work.

3. Place the new right cord to the left and over the filler cords, making sure to hold onto the original short cord as shown.

4. Finish the second part of the square knot by threading the new left working cord over the right working cord, behind the filler cords and up through the right side of the square knot.

5. Pull tight. When your piece is finished, sew the ends of the cords by using a large-eye needle and inserting them into the knots on the back of the work.

5

ADDING A CORD BY TYING A DOUBLE HALF HITCH

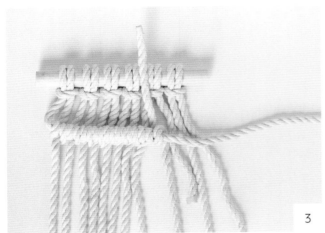

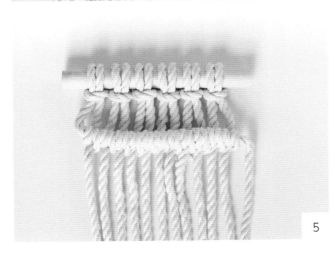

ADDING A CORD BY TYING A DOUBLE HALF HITCH

1. Where you're running out of rope, leave the working cord behind the filler cord.

2. Run the new cord behind the filler cord, so it's next to the rope you are replacing.

3. Wrap the new cord around the filler cord, tying a half hitch (page 17).

4. Tie another half hitch so that you've tied a double half hitch and place the cord behind.

5. Continue tying the rest of the cords as normal. When you have finished the piece, using a large-eye needle, sew the ends into the back of the knots.

ADDING A BEAD

Make sure the beads you plan on using have an interior diameter large enough to fit the diameter of cord you're using, and note whether they need to fit just one or two cords. It's easier to thread the cord through the beads if you tape the ends first with masking tape. You can add a bead in between any knots and also use an overhand knot to hold the bead on.

ADDING A BEAD BETWEEN SQUARE KNOT SINNETS

1. Thread the bead through the 2 filler cords.

2. Continue tying the knots tight to the bead, holding it in place.

ADDING A BEAD BETWEEN SQUARE KNOT SINNETS

1

2

Wall hangings

Wall hangings are a great art alternative for the home. I believe that art and handmade items are one of the best ways to personalize a space, but when people typically think about art, they unintentionally limit themselves to paintings. There is a whole world of other mediums out there! I love having macramé wall hangings in my home because they showcase their own unique textures, lines and patterns. They're also one of my favorite things to make because the possibilities are endless and that potential excites me!

I enjoy teaching my students how to create macramé wall hangings, because after you learn the essential knots and patterns, it's easy to personalize and make it your own. There are so many different directions you can go with a macramé wall hanging that when I'm making one, I'm often inspired to create an entirely new piece halfway through a pattern and end up with new ideas for two pieces! I hope you are just as excited to start making the wall hangings in this chapter. I designed these projects to teach you different techniques and patterns that will look great on your wall and hopefully inspire you to feel confident to create your own works of art.

HALO WALL HANGING

This is a great beginner project to tackle when you're new to macramé. This gold ring wall hanging is simple but makes a big statement on the wall! When it comes to macramé, things don't always have to be complicated to look great. Its modern and geometric aesthetics come together perfectly to create a unique and eye-catching piece of art.

skill level: beginner

MATERIALS AND TOOLS
About 90 feet (27.5 m) of ⁵⁄₆₄-inch (2-mm) three-strand rope

1 gold ring, 10 inch (25 cm) diameter

KNOTS USED
Lark's head knot (page 12)

Square knot (page 14)

Double half hitch (page 17)

1. Cut 12 pieces of rope, each 90 inches (228 cm) long. Fold each piece in half and attach to the top of the gold ring with a lark's head knot. When attaching the rope, position the cords so there is an approximate ½-inch (1.3-cm) gap between each lark's head knot.

2. Tie 1 square knot with the middle 4 cords approximately 1 inch (2.5 cm) from the very top of the ring.

1

2

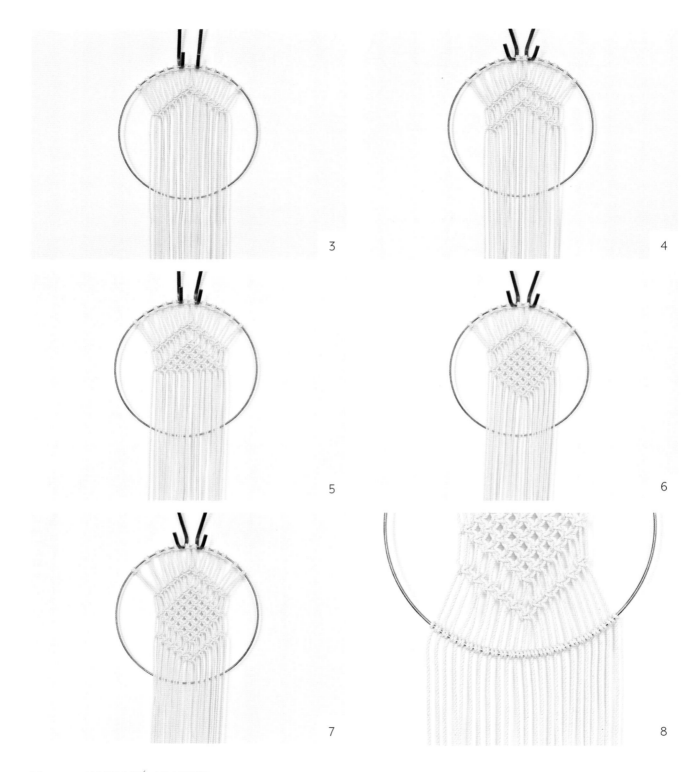

3

4

5

6

7

8

3. Tie 1 row of increasing alternating square knots, starting underneath the middle square knot and working your way left to the end of the ropes, and then do the same on the right. Be sure to tie the square knots tight to each other, leaving no space between each knot.

4. Leaving a 1-inch (2.5-cm) gap under the 1st row, repeat steps 2 and 3.

5. Tie alternating square knots, filling in the upside-down V you just made in step 4, leaving no space between each knot.

6. Tie 5 rows of decreasing alternating square knots, leaving no space between each knot, until you have 1 square knot remaining.

7. Leaving a 1-inch (2.5-cm) gap between the last square knots from step 6, tie 1 row of decreasing alternating square knots toward the middle rope on both sides. Continue to tie the square knots tight to each other, leaving no space between each knot.

8. Starting on the left, tie a double half hitch around the bottom of the gold ring, pulling each cord tight before tying each knot. Leave a gap of ⅛ inch (3 mm) between each double half hitch and continue across all of the ropes.

9. Trim the extra rope at the bottom of the wall hanging, straight across, to 15 inches (38 cm), or to your desired length.

10. Unravel the entire fringe and give it a final trim if desired.

variation

Try making your wall hanging with more negative space by leaving the center of your middle square knot diamond empty. Skip steps 5 and 6 and tie 1 row of decreasing alternating square knots, ending with 1 square knot to create an open diamond. Continue through the rest of the steps as written.

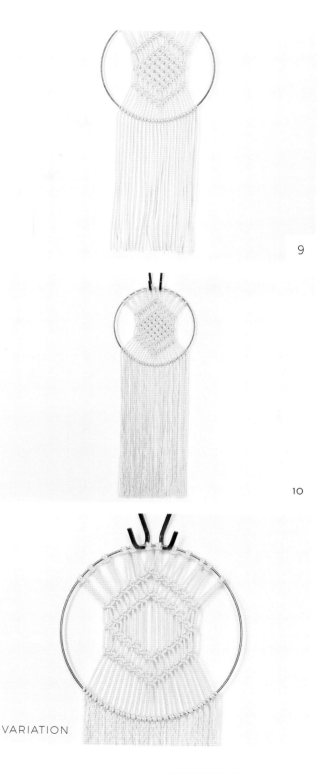

9

10

VARIATION

WILLOW WALL HANGING

If you're looking to add some beachy boho vibes to your space, then this is the wall hanging for you. The texture of the driftwood and macramé knots complement each other really well and make this a tactile showpiece. This project has so much versatility because the variation at the end of the instructions completely changes the look of the wall hanging from beachy boho to clean and modern. Both are beautiful in their own way, and who knows, you might just need both in your home!

Note: For the whole project, tie all left facing half knots.

skill level: beginner

MATERIALS AND TOOLS
About 109 feet (33.2 m) of ⅛-inch (3-mm) three-strand rope

Driftwood branch approximately 15 inches (38 cm) long

VARIATION
1½ x ¼ x 26½-inch (3.8 cm x 6 mm x 67.3-cm) piece of wood (I used oak)

Additional 59 feet (18 m) of ⅛-inch (3-mm) three-strand rope

KNOTS USED
Lark's head knot (page 12)

Continuous lark's head knot (page 32)

Half knot (page 13)

Double half hitch (page 17)

1. Cut one piece of rope 87 inches (221 cm) long. Measure 29 inches (73.7 cm) from one end and tie a lark's head knot to the left side of the branch. Take the longer side of the rope, measure 11 inches (28 cm) to hang below the branch and attach with a continuous lark's head knot to the right side of the branch. Let the right side of the rope hang down.

2. Cut 21 pieces of rope, each 58 inches (147 cm) long. Fold each piece in half and attach to the rope hanging below the branch with a lark's head knot. The 21 pieces should fill the rope hanging between each lark's head knot attached to the branch. If there is any extra space, adjust the lark's head knots tighter.

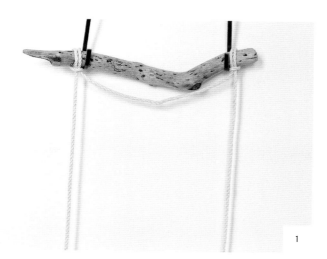

1

2

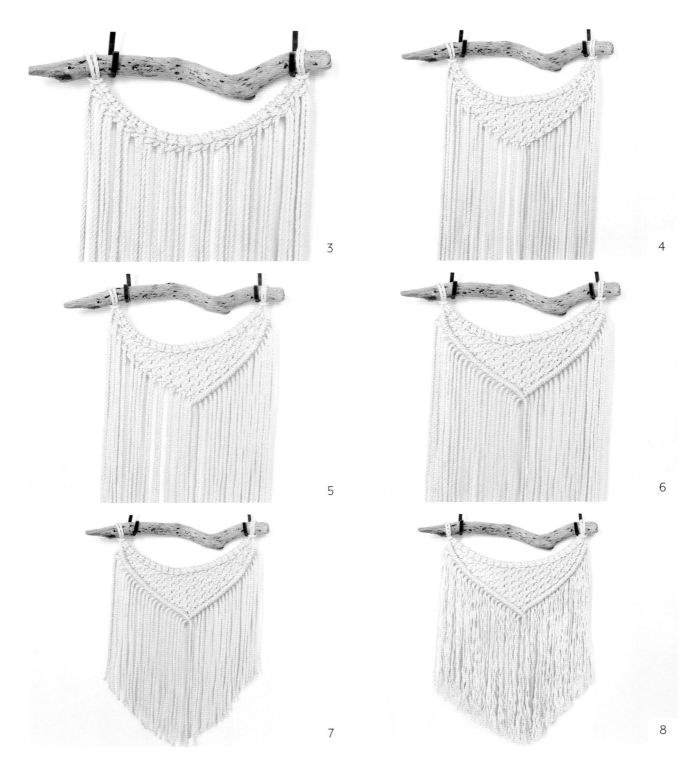

3

4

5

6

7

8

3. Tie a full row of half knots. Be sure to include the 2 cords hanging from either of the lark's head knots.

4. Continue tying decreasing alternating half knots until you have just 1 remaining half knot.

5. Starting on the right side, using the far right cord as the filler cord, tie 21 double half hitches tight to the half knots above, leaving no space between the knots.

6. Starting on the left side, using the far left cord as the filler cord, tie 22 double half hitches tight to the half knots above, leaving no space between the knots. For the 22nd double half hitch, use the filler cord from the right double half hitch to make a sharp point.

7. Matching the angle of the knots above, trim the rope at the bottom of the wall hanging to 10 inches (25.5 cm), or to your desired length.

8. Unravel the entire fringe and give it a final trim if desired.

variation

Change the look of this wall hanging by making two mini versions and adding them to either side of the centerpiece. Change the look even more by using a straight piece of wood or dowel instead of using driftwood. Complete steps 1–8 on the 1½ x ¼ x 26½-inch (3.8 cm x 6 mm x 67.3-cm) piece of wood. Cut 2 pieces of rope 58 inches (147 cm) long. Attach both pieces of rope using continuous lark's head knots on either side of the middle piece, the same way you did in step 1. Leave 3½ inches (9 cm) in between each lark's head knot. Cut 14 pieces of rope 42 inches (106.5 cm) long. On both sides, attach 7 pieces to the 3½-inch (9-cm) piece of hanging rope. On both sides, tie 4 rows of decreasing alternating half knots until you reach 1 half knot. On both sides, tie diagonal half hitches on either side of the alternating half hitches, ending in a point. Trim and unravel your fringe as desired.

VARIATION

CLASSIC GARLAND

This project is so versatile and can hang almost anywhere—on the wall, from a mantle or shelf, or over a bed, couch or window. Unlike some wall hangings, the way in which this one hangs can be adjusted, by changing the length of rope you use in step 1. My hope is that this project shows you that you don't need a branch or dowel to make a macramé piece. You can be just as creative with only rope!

skill level: beginner

MATERIALS AND TOOLS
About 273½ feet (83.4 m) of 3⁄16-inch (5-mm) three-strand rope

KNOTS USED
Overhand knot (page 18)

Lark's head knot (page 12)

Square knot (page 14)

Double half hitch (page 17)

Gathering knot (page 19)

1. Cut 1 piece of rope 63 inches (160 cm) long. This will be what you attach your other rope to. Measure 12 inches (30.5 cm) in from one end and within that space tie an overhand knot leaving a 1½-inch (3.8-cm) loop. Do this on the other side. Trim the extra tail of rope close to the knot you just tied.

2. Cut 40 pieces of rope 67 inches (170 cm) long. Leaving approximately 2½ inches (6.3 cm) of space on either side from the overhand knots, attach the ropes using a lark's head knot to the rope from step 1.

1

2

3

4

5

6

3. Section off the hanging ropes into 5 sections, with 16 strands of rope in each section. In each section, tie 3 square knots with the middle 12 pieces of rope, leaving 2 pieces of rope on either side. Then tie decreasing alternating square knots, ending with 1 square knot in each section.

4. Still working section by section, tie a diagonal double half hitch on the left and the right side of each decreasing alternating square knot section, ending with a point (page 27). Do this to each of the 5 sections.

5. In between each section, take 8 cords from the middle and tie a cluster of 4 square knots (page 14). Leaving a ⅛-inch (3-mm) gap directly under the double half hitches, tie 1 square knot in the 1st row, 2 alternating square knots on the 2nd row and 1 square knot centered on the 3rd row. Do this 4 times in between each section. With the first 4 and last 4 cords on the far left and right side of the garland, just tie 1 square knot.

6. With the remaining cords underneath each section from step 4, tie a diagonal double half hitch with no space in between the previous row, ending in a point. Do this to 3 of the 5 sections (the 1st, 3rd and 5th sections).

7

8

7. Cut 2 pieces of rope 32 inches (81 cm) long. There's no need to tape the ends of these pieces. With both pieces of rope, separate the 3 strands of rope so that you have 6 pieces to work with. Under each small cluster of 4 alternating square knots (including the single square knots on both ends from step 5), using one of the 6 pieces you just separated, tie a gathering knot that is ½ to ¾ inch (1.3 to 2 cm) wide. You are tying a total of 6 gathering knots.

8. Trim the extra rope at the bottom of the wall hanging to 11 inches (28 cm), or to your desired length. Note: If some pieces ended up a little shorter than 11 inches (28 cm), it's ok! Step 9 will help blend them all together.

9. Unravel the entire fringe and give it a final trim if desired.

9

variation

If you want a fuller look to this bunting banner, leave out step 7. Continue to unravel the entire fringe as you normally would.

VARIATION

PALM FROND WALL HANGING

I really enjoyed designing this leaf wall hanging because it was so different not working off of a dowel or a ring. This solid-looking piece is free-hanging, meaning that it hangs on its own without any assistance from rope or wood. I love styling either variation of this leaf on a wall surrounded by a few other favorite art pieces or as part of a gallery wall. It's the perfect way to break up geometric frames and art with a textural piece that has a unique shape.

skill level: intermediate

MATERIALS AND TOOLS

About 174 feet (53 m) of ³⁄₁₆-inch (5-mm) three-strand rope

Large eye needle

VARIATION

About 374 feet (114 m) of ⁵⁄₆₄-inch (2-mm) three-strand rope

KNOTS USED

Overhand knot (page 18)

Double half hitch (page 17)

Vertical Double Half Hitch (page 36)

Gathering knot (page 19)

1. Cut 1 piece of rope 124 inches (315 cm) long, and cut 15 pieces 126 inches (320 cm) long. Using the 124-inch (315-cm) piece, fold it in half, and tie 1 overhand knot in the middle.

2. Using 1 of the 126-inch (320-cm) cords, from the center, tie 1 double half hitch on the right side of the overhand knot. On the left side of the overhand knot, tie another double half hitch with the same 126-inch (320-cm) cord. Tie the 2nd double half hitch tight to the other, leaving no space between each knot. This is a similar technique to tying vertical double half hitches (page 36).

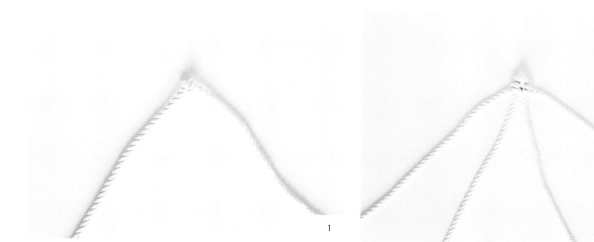

1

2

3

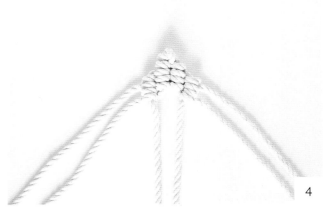

4

5

3. Using another 126-inch (320-cm) cord, repeat step 2, tying the double half hitches beside the other double half hitch.

4. On both sides, tie a row of double half hitches with the ropes from the previous row, using the top rope as the filler cord.

5. Add another 126-inch (320-cm) cord; from the middle of that cord, tie 1 double half hitch on the right side cord, next to the other double half hitches. Using the left side of the 126-inch (320-cm) cord, tie another double half hitch tight to the other, leaving no space between each knot. This connects the rows.

6. Repeat steps 4 and 5, 11 times.

6

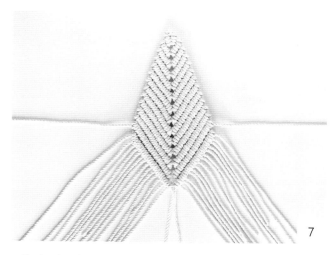
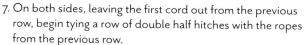
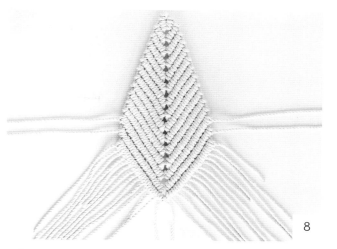

7

8

7. On both sides, leaving the first cord out from the previous row, begin tying a row of double half hitches with the ropes from the previous row.

8. Repeat step 7. With your last knot, tie a double half hitch, ending in a sharp point.

9. Cut 1 piece of rope 72 inches (183 cm) long. Gathering the bottom 6 cords together, tie a gathering knot around them approximately 2¾ inches (7 cm) wide. Trim the excess rope from the gathering knot.

10. Trim and unravel the remaining cords of rope, then use a large-eye needle to sew each strand into the back of the leaf and trim.

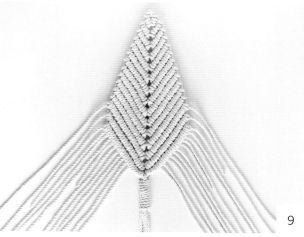

9

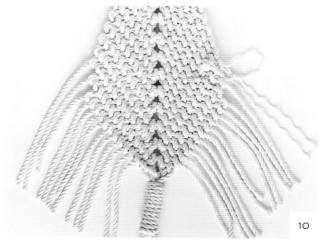

10

11. When finished, the strands should all be neatly hidden on the back of the palm frond.

12. Give the stem a final trim 6 inches (15 cm) below the gathering knot. Unravel the ropes and give a final trim if desired. To hang, simply place it on a nail in the wall between rows near the top of the leaf!

variation

Repeat the pattern with a smaller size rope to change the size of your leaf! Using ⁵⁄₆₄-inch (2-mm) rope, cut 1 piece 84 inches (213 cm) long and 6 pieces 43 inches (109 cm) long; cut the gathering knot piece 32 inches (81 cm) long. Continue through the pattern as written.

11

12

WOVEN WALL HANGING

I really enjoyed designing this project because it brought the art of braiding and macramé together to create an intricate wall hanging in a fun way. My favorite part of making this project was braiding the twelve strands together to add a unique texture that complements any space. I hope you enjoy the process as much as I did! See final image on the next page.

skill level: intermediate

MATERIALS AND TOOLS
About 196 feet (60 m) of ⁵⁄₆₄-inch (2-mm) three-strand rope

About 29 inches (74 cm) of ¹⁄₁₆-inch (1.5-mm) three-strand rope or any thin rope or string

2 wooden dowels, ⁷⁄₁₆ inch (1 cm) wide, 17¼ inches (44 cm) long

1 wooden ring, 1¼ inches (3 cm) diameter

Large-eye needle

KNOTS USED
Lark's head knot (page 12)

Square knot sinnet (page 22)

Double half hitch (page 17)

Overhand knot (page 18)

1. Using the ⁵⁄₆₄-inch (2-mm) three-strand rope, cut 24 pieces 98 inches (249 cm) long. Attach each piece to one of the wooden dowels with a lark's head knot. When attaching the rope, position the cords so there is a working cord on either side of 2 filler cords, adjusting the lengths so that the working cords are longer than the filler cords. The filler cords should be 25 inches (63.5 cm) long. For example, the order starting from the left would be 1 working cord, 2 filler cords, 1 working cord, 1 working cord, 2 filler cords, 1 working cord, and so on.

2. Tie 28 square knot sinnets on each of the 12 sections. This makes each strand of sinnets approximately 11 inches (28 cm) long.

1

2

A · B · C · D · E · F · G · H · I · J · K · L

A · B · C · D · E · G · F · H · I · J · K · L

3

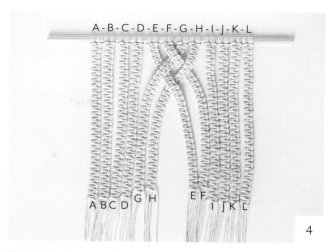

A · B · C · D · E · F · G · H · I · J · K · L

A B C D G H E F I J K L

4

3. Lay your piece on the floor so it is easier to braid. Begin braiding with the 12 square knot sinnets. Cross cord F over cord G.

4. Cross cord H over F. Cross cord E under G and over H.

5. Cross cord D over G and under H. Cross cord I under F and over E. Cross cord D over I.

6. Weave J over F, under E and over D. Weave C under G, over H, under I and over J.

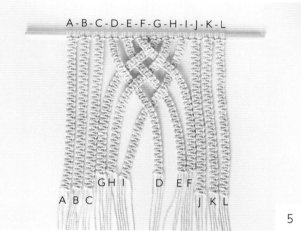

A · B · C · D · E · F · G · H · I · J · K · L

A B C G H I D E F J K L

5

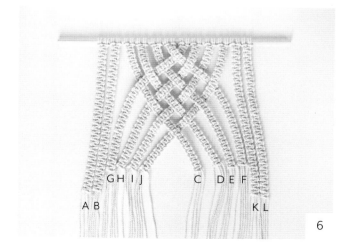

G H I J C D E F

A B K L

6

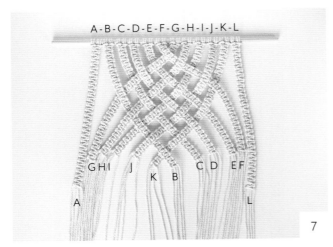

A-B-C-D-E-F-G-H-I-J-K-L

GHI J CD EF
K B
A L

7

A-B-C-D-E-F-G-H-I-J-K-L

GH I J KL AB CDEF

8

7. Weave B over and under the strands until you get to the end. Weave K over and under the strands until you get to the end.

8. Weave L over and under the strands until you get to the end. Weave A over and under the strands until you get to the end.

9. If needed, shift the sinnets around so that they all end at about the same spot. Tie each cord with a double half hitch around the second dowel.

10. Using the 1⁄16-inch (1.5-mm) rope, cut a 29-inch (74-cm) piece. Fold it in half and tie a lark's head knot around the wooden ring. Make sure the front of the lark's head knot is facing the front of the wall hanging. Flip both the wooden ring and the wall hanging so the back is facing up.

9

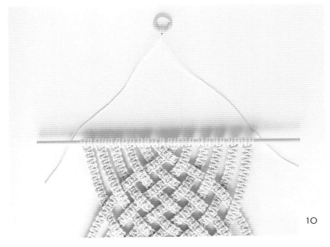

10

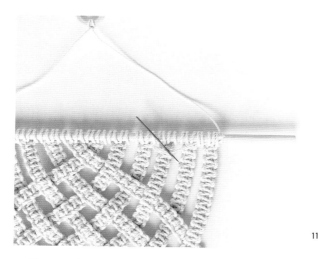

11

12

11. Tie 2 overhand knots around both sides of the dowel and position the knot at the back of the wall hanging. Using a large-eye needle, sew in the ends of the 2 knots you just tied into the back of 2 of the lark's head knots. Cut off the extra rope.

12. Trim the extra rope at the bottom of the wall hanging to 10 inches (25.5 cm), or to your desired length.

13. Unravel the entire fringe and give it a final trim if needed.

variation

Try using relatively straight "found" branches or drift wood instead of the dowels to give this project a unique, natural look. Also, for this variation to look best, skip steps 10 and 11, to keep all the wooden elements natural. Note: If you are using thicker branches than the dowels, this could slightly affect your total length of rope. To account for this, add 5 to 10 inches (12.5 to 25.5 cm) more, depending on the thickness of the branches.

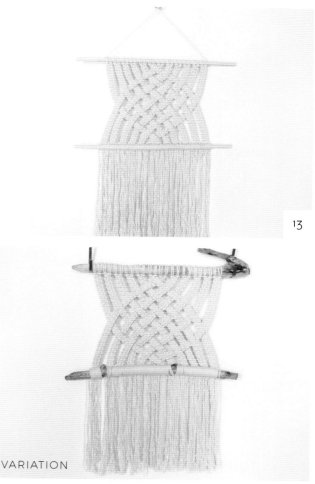

13

VARIATION

PAVÉ DIAMOND WALL HANGING

The double half hitch is one of my favorite knots, and its prominence in this piece makes this wall hanging so beautiful! This project is a bit of a throwback to the retro feel of macramé from the 1970s, but with a modern twist. What I really love about it is the intricacy within the repeating patterns. Like a lot of the wall hanging projects in this book, the dowel that this piece hangs from can be swapped out for a straight piece of driftwood.

skill level: advanced

MATERIALS AND TOOLS

About 366 feet (111.6 m) of ⁵⁄₆₄-inch (2-mm) three-strand rope

Wooden dowel, ½ inch (1.3 cm) wide, approximately 17 inches (43 cm) long

Large-eye needle

KNOTS USED

Lark's head knot (page 12)

Double half hitch (page 17)

Square knot (page 14)

Open diamond pattern (page 38)

1. Cut 24 pieces of rope 15 feet (4.6 m) long, and cut 3 pieces of rope 24 inches (61 cm) long. With a lark's head knot, attach the 24 pieces of 15-foot (4.6-m) rope to the dowel, centering them.

2. Using one of the 24-inch (61-cm) pieces of rope as the filler cord, leave a tail of 6 inches (15 cm) and tie a full row of horizontal double half hitches with each of the cords. Tie the double half hitches leaving no space between the dowel and knots.

3

4

5a

3. Tie a full row of square knots tight to the row above, totaling 12 square knots.

4. Repeat step 2 with another length of 24-inch (61-cm) rope.

5. Part A) Divide the 48 cords into 3 sections, with 16 cords in each section. In each section, tie an open diamond pattern with 2 rows of double half hitches. Do not connect the very first and last rows of open diamonds. Halfway through the diamond, tie a square knot in the middle with 1 working cord and 8 filler cords. Be careful to keep the filler cords flat, side by side and not overlapping.

Part B) Complete the bottom of the open diamond with two rows of double half hitches.

5b

6

7

6. Repeat step 2 with the last length of 24-inch (61-cm) rope. Begin the double half hitch row by leaving a 1-inch (2.5-cm) gap with the first and last cord from the diamonds.

7. Repeat both parts of step 5a and b.

8. Leaving the first 8 and last 8 cords out, tie an open diamond pattern, this time connecting the first and the last rows with a point, as shown on page 37. Leave a 1½-inch (3.8-cm) gap between the previous row of open diamonds.

9. Leaving the first 16 and last 16 cords out, tie the same open diamond pattern from step 8. Leave the same 1½-inch (3.8-cm) gap between the previous row of open diamonds.

8

9

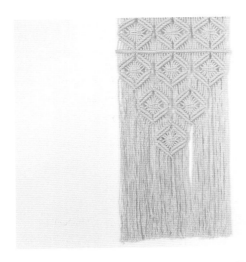

10. Cut the ropes to your desired length and then unravel all of the cords from the center diamond. Unravel the rest of the cords, leaving 2½ inches (6 cm) of rope together under the rest of the diamonds.

11. Unravel the ends of the filler cords from the horizontal rows of double half hitches from steps 2, 4 and 6. With the large-eye needle, sew the unraveled strands into the back of the knots. Trim off the excess rope.

variation

Instead of tying diamonds, try tying this wall hanging with open X's (page 38).

10

11

VARIATION

LINEA GARLAND

I love this more advanced garland! The combination of positive and negative space with linear directional patterns is delightful to the eye and a unique accent for any room. Like the beginner garland project, this more advanced version looks great hung on the wall, from a mantle or a shelf, or over a bed, window or couch. Wherever you hang it in your home, this statement piece is sure to get a lot of positive comments from guests!

skill level: advanced

MATERIALS AND TOOLS
About 550½ feet (167.8 m) of ⅛-inch (3-mm) three-strand rope

KNOTS USED
Overhand knot (page 18)

Lark's head knot (page 12)

Square knot (page 14)

Double half hitch (page 17)

Square knot sinnet pine tree pattern (page 23)

Reef knot (page 18)

Gathering knot (page 19)

Variation: Weaving pattern (page 21)

1. Cut 1 piece of rope 68 inches (172.7 cm) long. This will be what you attach your other ropes to. Measure approximately 10 inches (25.5 cm) in from one end and tie an overhand knot with a loop within that space. Do this on the other side. Trim the extra tail of rope close to the knot you just tied.

2. Cut 70 pieces of rope 90 inches (229 cm) long. Fold each piece in half and attach to the rope from step 1 with a lark's head knot, leaving approximately 2½ inches (6 cm) of space on either side from the overhand knot.

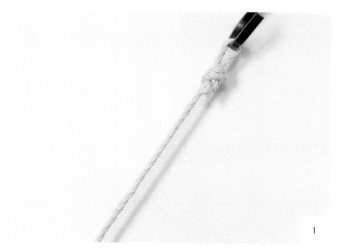

1

2

3

4

3. Divide the rope into 5 sections, with 28 strands of rope in each section. Working in one section, tie decreasing alternating square knots starting with 7 square knots in the 1st row and ending with 1. Complete this for each of the 5 sections.

4. Still working section by section, tie a diagonal double half hitch under the left side of each decreasing alternating square knot section, tight to the knots above. Do this to each of the 5 sections.

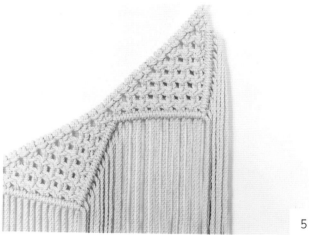

5

5. Still working section by section, use the first rope coming out from the left side of the double half hitch as the filler cord and tie diagonal double half hitches under the right side of each decreasing alternating square knot section. Do this to each of the 5 sections. To tie a point, use the right side's filler cord as the working cord and tie a double half hitch to continue the left side's row of double half hitches. Do this for each of the 5 sections.

6. Working in between each of the 5 sections, take the 8 middle cords and tie a square knot with 1 working cord and 6 filler cords. Do this in each of the 4 middle sections.

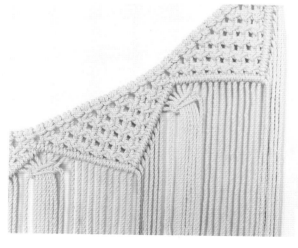

6

7

8

9

10

7. Still working in the 4 middle sections, use the 6th cord on each side of the filler cord and tie double half hitches with the 5th cord and the corresponding cords from the square knot. To tie the point, use the right filler cord as the working cord on the left side for the double half hitch.

8. In all 4 sections, under the row from step 7, leaving no space, tie 1 row of 3 decreasing alternating square knots, ending with 1 square knot.

9. In the far right section, using the working cord from the first square knot from step 8, make this the filler cord and tie diagonal double half hitches (angling right) tight to the row above. On the right side of the section, with the 8th cord, tie a row tight to the row above of diagonal double half hitches (angling left), ending with a point. Do this to the far left section, in reverse. In the remaining 3 sections, still using the working cord from the first square knot from step 8, tie diagonal double half hitches (angling inward), ending with a point.

10. In each of the 5 sections below step 9, leaving 2 cords out on each side, tie 1 row on each side of diagonal double half hitches, ending with a point. Leave no space between rows.

11

12

11. Under the square knot from step 8, tie a square knot sinnet pine tree pattern, consisting of 5 square knots, using new working cords from the square knots above each time. Place the working cords behind after each knot. Do this under each of the 4 middle sections.

12. Using the cords you placed behind after tying each square knot from step 11, tie another square knot sinnet pine tree pattern around the 2 cords under the point of the double half hitch. Tie a total of 7 square knots in a sinnet, using a new working cord each time. Complete this in each of the 3 sections.

13. When tying the last pine tree pattern square knot sinnets on the far left side and right side, work your way using the cords on the left and right edges from the outside in, top to bottom. Refer to the photo.

14. With the remaining 12 cords from opposite sections, tie the first step of a reef knot loosely, as pictured. Do this a total of 5 times.

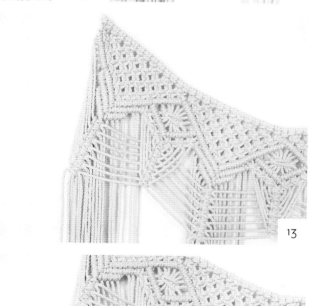

13

14

15

15. Cut 9 pieces of rope 34 inches (86 cm) long. Gather together the ropes from step 14 and arrange the cords from the reef knot so they lie neatly beside each other. Tie a gathering knot, using the cord you just cut, around the ropes just under the overhand knot. Complete this in each of the 4 sections. Trim the excess rope. Using another piece of the 34-inch (86-cm) rope, gather together the ropes under the square knot sinnet in one section and tie a gathering knot right below the last square knot. Complete this in each of the 4 remaining sections. Trim the excess rope.

16. Trim each tassel to approximately 10 inches (25.5 cm) long, measuring from below the gathering knot.

17. Unravel the rope from each tassel and trim again if desired.

variation

Try weaving the cords over and under each other instead of tying a square knot from step 7. See the weaving pattern on page 21.

16

17

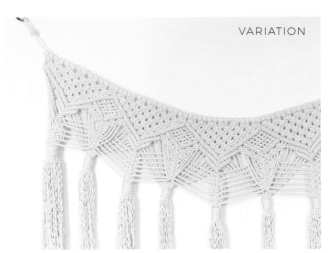

VARIATION

MOSAIC WALL HANGING

Who doesn't love a large statement piece?! Whether you hang it above a couch or bed, or fill out an empty wall with it, this wall hanging will grab everyone's attention. I hope you enjoy the process of working on a large piece and the pride you'll feel when you finish. As this is an advanced piece, don't push yourself to try and finish it in one sitting. Be sure to take breaks and stretch so that you don't get worn out. Macramé is deceptively tough on your body in long stretches!

Note: For the whole project, tie all knots tight to each other, with no space between each row, unless otherwise stated.

skill level: advanced

MATERIALS AND TOOLS
About 759 feet (232 m) of ³⁄₁₆-inch (5-mm) three-strand rope

Wooden piece 1 x 2 x 50 inches (2.5 x 5 x 127 cm)

VARIATION
About 120 additional feet (36.5 m) of ³⁄₁₆-inch (5-mm) three-strand rope

Wood piece 1 x 2 x 70 inches (2.5 x 5 x 178 cm)

KNOTS USED
Lark's head knot (page 18)

Double half hitch (page 17)

Square knot (page 14)

Square knot sinnet (page 22)

Gathering knot (page 19)

1. Cut 34 pieces of rope 16 feet (4.9 m) long, and cut 22 pieces of rope 13 feet (3.9 m) long. Attach all 56 pieces of rope to the piece of wood using a lark's head knot. Attach the long pieces in the middle of the wood and half of the shorter pieces on either side of the longer pieces.

2. Counting 42 ropes in from the left, tie a diagonal double half hitch, using the 42nd cord as the filler cord (angling left). Tie a total of 14 double half hitches. Repeat the same step on the right side, angling to the right instead.

1

2

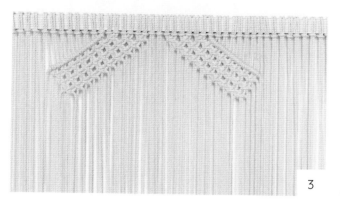

3

4

3. Tie 3 square knots to the right of the first double half hitches you just tied in step 2. Continue tying 3 rows of alternating square knots directly under the double half hitch of step 2. Then on the right side of the wall hanging, do the reverse, tying 3 square knots to the left of the double half hitch. Continue tying 3 rows of alternating square knots. In the row closest to the outside of the wall hanging, there will be 8 square knots in the row, then moving inward, 9 square knots and then 10.

4. With the center 4 cords, use the 2nd cord from the left as the filler cord and tie 22 diagonal double half hitches, angling to the right, ending in the same spot from steps 2 and 3. Then use the first working cord from the first double half hitches from the beginning of this step as the filler cord. Tie 21 double half hitches tight to the alternating square knots, angling left, ending in the same spot as in step 3.

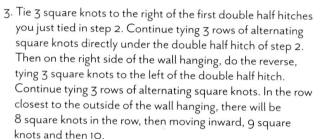
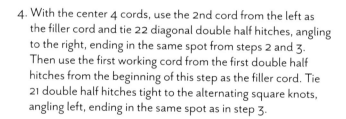

5

5. Leaving a space of 1¼ inches (3 cm), tie 1 square knot in the very center of the wall hanging, under the half diamond of double half hitches. Leaving the same 1¼-inch (3-cm) space, tie 1 row of 8 alternating square knots on both sides, angling outwards.

6. Now turn your wall hanging around so you are looking at the back. Start by tying a double half hitch point in the middle, then tie 1 row of diagonal half hitches under both sides of the 2 rows of square knots from step 5, leaving a very small gap of about ⅛ inch (3 mm).

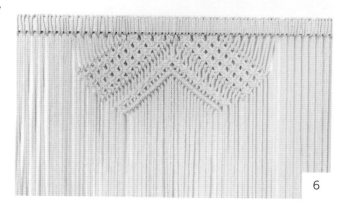

6

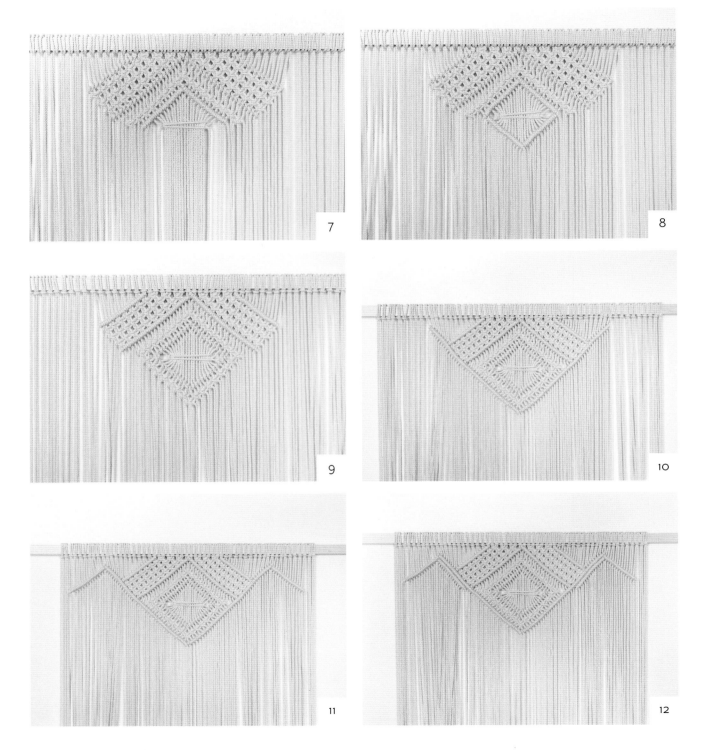

7. Tie 1 large square knot with 1 working cord and 18 filler cords. Arrange the cords so they are lying flat and side by side (not bunched up).

8. Using the working cord coming out of the last double half hitch as the filler cord, tie 11 double half hitches on the right side and 12 on the left side, joining them with a double half hitch (making a point).

9. Flip your wall hanging back around so you are looking at the front again. On both sides, leaving the same ⅛-inch (3-mm) gap, tie 1 row of 7 alternating square knots underneath your last square knot from step 5, angling in toward the center. Finish the diamond by tying both together with 1 centered square knot.

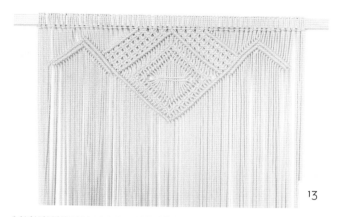

13

10. On the left side of the wall hanging, count in 19 cords; leaving a space of 1 inch (2.5 cm) from the top, tie a row of diagonal double half hitches angling toward the middle. Tie a total of 37 diagonal double half hitches. Do the same on the other side, tying a total of 37 double half hitches. Tie a point with the right cord over the left side's filler cord.

11. On both sides, tie a row of diagonal double half hitches angling outward, around the filler cord from the first double half hitch from the previous step. Tie a total of 14 double half hitches. The row should end about 5½ inches (14 cm) from the wooden piece.

12. On both sides, starting with the cord coming from the first double half hitch from the previous step, tie 14 diagonal double half hitches around that cord, angling inward.

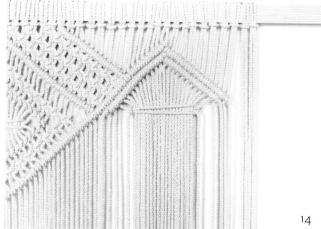

14

13. On both sides, starting with the cord coming from the first double half hitch from the previous step, tie 12 diagonal double half hitches around that cord, angling outward.

14. On both sides, tie a large square knot using one working cord around 20 filler cords. Arrange the cords so they are lying flat side by side (not bunched up).

15. On both sides, using the cord from the last double half hitch from step 12, tie 13 diagonal double half hitches, angling outward.

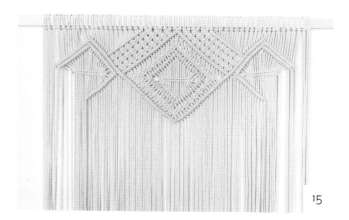

15

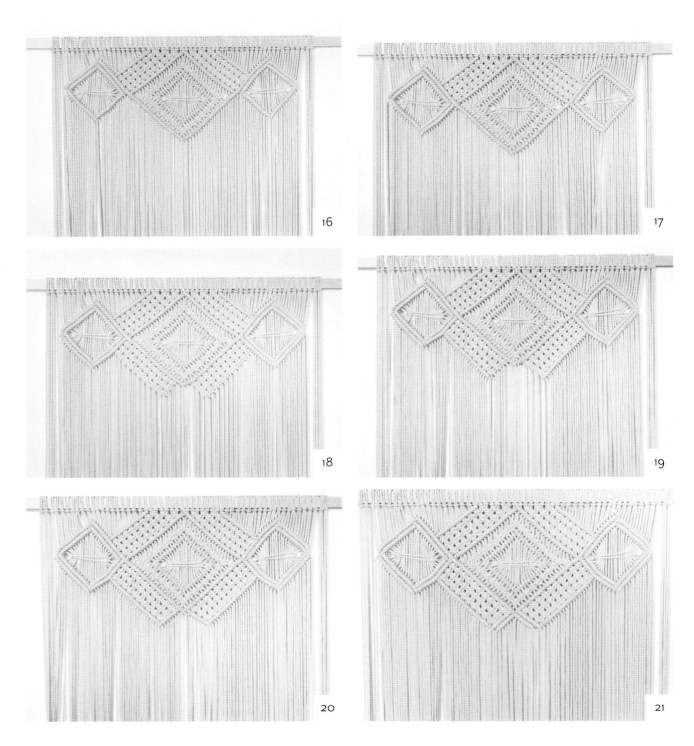

16

17

18

19

20

21

16. On both sides, using the filler cord from the last double half hitch from step 13, tie 12 diagonal double half hitches, angling inward and using the corresponding cords, making sure not to crisscross any.

17. On both sides, using the same filler cord from step 4, tie 14 double half hitches, following the same angle from step 4.

18. On both sides, using the same filler cord from step 11, turn the filler cord at a 90-degree angle (inward) and begin tying 15 diagonal double half hitches.

    Then, on both sides, starting from the corner created by steps 10 and 17, tie 3 rows of 10 decreasing alternating square knots following the angle from step 10.

19. On both sides, under the last row of alternating square knots, tie 20 diagonal double half hitches angling inwards.

20. On both sides, using the last cords from the second to last double half hitches from step 10, tie 7 double half hitches under the row of alternating square knots, angling outward.

21. On both sides, in the very middle of the wall hanging, tie 6 double half hitches, extending the rows created in step 10.

22. Tie a square knot with 1 working cord and 8 filler cords. Make sure all of the filler cords are lying side by side (not bunched up).

23. On both sides, complete the diamond of double half hitches around the square knot you just tied from the previous step. Use the cord from the last double half hitch from step 21 to be the filler cord. Tie 5 diagonal double half hitches on the right side and 6 on the left side, making a point. This is similar to tying a diamond with sharp corners (page 37).

24. On both sides, continue the row of double half hitches from step 19, tying 6 on the right side and 7 on the left side, making a point.

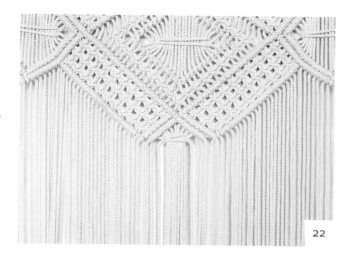

22

23

24

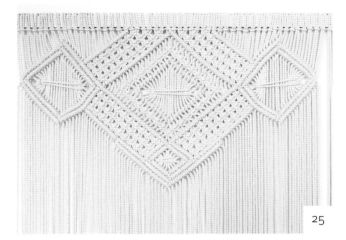

25

26

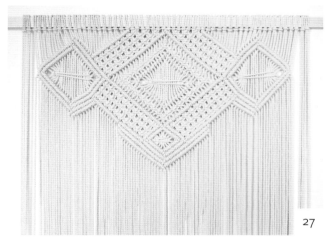

27

25. On both sides, counting 11 cords down from the corner from steps 17 and 19, use the 12th cord as the filler cord and tie 17 diagonal double half hitches on the left side and 16 on the right side, ending with a point.

26. On both sides, using the cord from the first double half hitch tied in the previous step, tie 16 diagonal double half hitches on the right side and 17 on the left side, ending in a point.

27. On both sides, using the 1st and 2nd cords from the top corner of step 19, tie 2 rows of 8 diagonal double half hitches.

28. With the 4 cords left on both sides of the wall hanging, tie a row of square knot sinnets, 9 square knots long.

28

29. Cut 2 pieces of rope 36 inches (91 cm) long. Tie a gathering knot 1¾ inches (4.5 cm) wide around the 4 cords from the square knot sinnets.

30. Trim the cords at your desired length following the angle of the knots. Unravel all of the cords and square knot sinnet tassels and trim again if desired.

variation

Make this wall hanging larger on a 1 x 2 x 70-inch (2.5 x 5 x 178-cm) piece of wood by adding the steps below after completing the entire wall hanging and all of the steps. Although there are several additional steps here, they are very similar to the project itself, so feel free to go back and reference the step-by-step photos from earlier in the project.

Cut 28 pieces of rope 8 feet (2.5 m) long. For the following steps, do the same on both sides of the wall hanging. Attach 14 pieces on either side using a lark's head knot. Tie a square knot sinnet consisting of 8 square knots with the 4 end cords. In the middle of the 12 cords, tie 2 rows of 6 increasing alternating square knots. Tie 2 rows of diagonal double half hitches to the edge of both sides. Be sure to mimic the corners intersecting the two diamonds on either side of the main wall hanging. Tie a large square knot with 1 working cord and 16 filler cords in the middle of the half diamond. Finish the diamond with 2 diagonal double half hitch rows, both ending in a point. Cut 2 pieces of rope 44½ inches (113 cm) long. Tie a gathering knot at the base of the square knot sinnet on either end. Cut the ropes in a diamond shape, mimicking the angle from the bottom of the diamond.

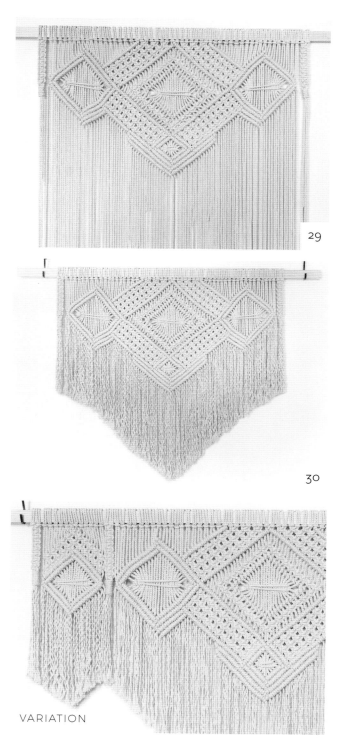

29

30

VARIATION

plant hangers

If you were to walk through my house, you wouldn't be surprised to find out that one of the first macramé pieces I ever made was a plant hanger. I'm unapologetically addicted to filling every room of my house with plants, and to be honest, it's beginning to look like a jungle in there! Not only do plants add a pop of color and life to a space, but also some plants even purify the air, increase productivity and boost your mood. However, with all those plants comes the need to showcase them in unique ways. Macramé plant hangers are such a beautiful way to show off your plants and make them a focal point in your home. I like to bring plants up off the floor or tables and into my line of sight, and for households with pets or children, getting plants out of the way can be vital to their survival! I know in my home, macramé plant hangers have saved countless plants from my three cats.

Plant hangers are versatile because there are so many ways to make them, and these projects are designed to accommodate a wide variety of hanging plants, from hanging vines to tiny succulents. Some of my favorite go-to hanging plants that are also easy to care for are pothos, heart-shaped philodendrons, ivy vines and spider plants. I also love string of pearls and donkey tail succulents, which trail down. They require a little more care and observation, but are definitely worth it!

PETITE TIERED PLANT HANGER

There's something about small or mini things that makes them the cutest! This plant hanger perfectly complements small potted plants like tiny cactuses and succulents as well as any small hanging plants. I love filling my house with both of those types of plants because they don't take up a lot of room, which makes this project especially great if you live in a small space.

skill level: beginner

MATERIALS AND TOOLS
About 58 feet (17.7 m) of ⅟₁₆-inch (1.5-mm) three-strand rope

1 small wooden ring (ring shown has an interior diameter of 1 inch [2.5 cm])

KNOTS USED
Gathering knot (page 19)

Half knot sinnet (page 24)

Square knot (page 14)

1. Cut 3 pieces of rope 144 inches (366 cm) long and 3 pieces of rope 72 inches (183 cm) long. Thread both lengths of rope through the wooden ring, placing the ring in the center of both lengths of rope. Cut 1 piece of rope 16 inches (40.5 cm) long. Tie a gathering knot ½ inch (1.3 cm) wide right under the ring. Trim the excess rope from the gathering knot.

2. Divide the rope into 3 sections, pairing 2 long strands with 2 short strands in each group. Within each section, position the 2 long cords as the working cords and the shorter 2 cords as the filler cords. Tie 21 half knots, making a 2¾-inch (7-cm) half knot sinnet in all 3 sections.

1

2

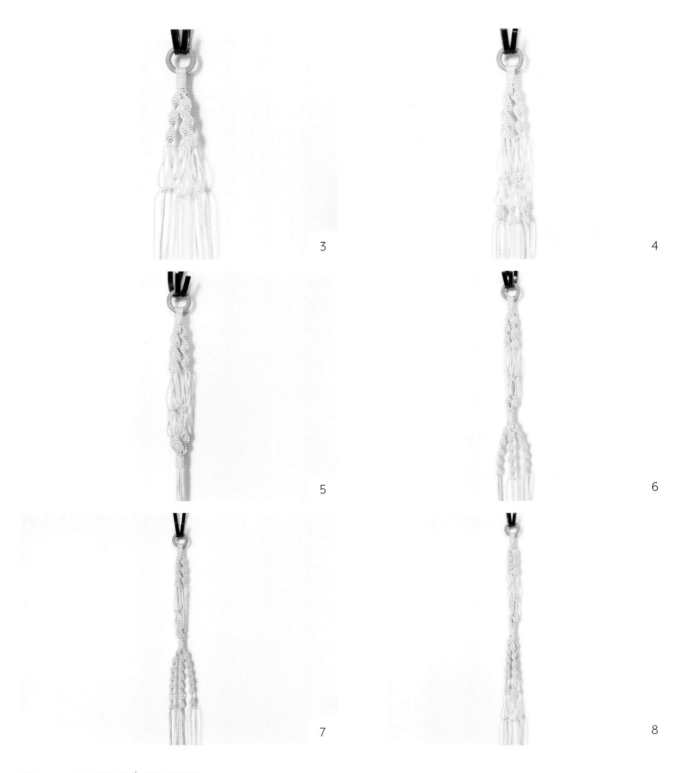

3

4

5

6

7

8

3. Leave a space of 2 inches (5 cm) and tie a square knot by alternating the working and filler cords. Making each working cord a filler cord and each filler cord a working cord, create 3 new sections.

4. Position the cords in their original groups from step 2. Leaving a 1¼-inch (3-cm) space, tie 8 half knots, making a 1-inch (2.5-cm) half knot sinnet.

5. Cut 1 piece of rope 16 inches (40.5 cm) long. Leave a ¼-inch (6-mm) gap and tie a gathering knot ½ inch (1.3 cm) wide around all 12 cords. Trim the excess rope from the gathering knot.

6. Divide the rope into 3 sections, pairing 2 long strands with 2 short strands in each group. Within each section position the 2 long cords as the working cords and the shorter 2 cords as the filler cords. Tie 34 half knots, making a 3¾-inch (9.5-cm) half knot sinnet in all 3 sections.

7. In all 3 sections, leave a ½-inch (1.3-cm) gap and tie 8 half knots, making a 1-inch (2.5-cm) half knot sinnet.

8. Leaving a 2¾-inch (7-cm) space, repeat step 3.

9. Leaving a 1½-inch (3.8-cm) gap, repeat step 4.

10. Cut 1 piece of rope 28 inches (71 cm) long and tie a gathering knot 1 inch (2.5 cm) wide. Trim the excess rope from the gathering knot.

11. Trim 8½ inches (21.5 cm) below the gathering knot. Unravel the ropes if desired. I chose to leave mine intact.

variation

Make a mini single plant hanger by completing step 1 and skipping down to step 6. Complete the rest of the steps to finish the plant hanger as written. (See page 94 for image.)

9

10

11

CASCADE PLANT HANGER

Even though I love small, complex details, I do believe that sometimes—and you won't hear me say this often—simplicity really is best. Occasionally, adding something simple to a space is exactly what it needs. These subtle arrows add a lovely directional movement to this plant hanger, pointing to the star of the show, the plant! Using the sleek and modern-looking braided rope adds to the clean simplicity of the piece. Another great thing about this plant hanger is that it hangs flat to your wall and can be used to bring life and a splash of greenery to a space. I would choose a pothos plant or heart-shaped philodendron for this hanger because their full, cascading leaves contrast with the small details in the macramé.

skill level: beginner

MATERIALS AND TOOLS
About 83 feet (25.3 m) of ⅛-inch (3-mm) braided (or awning) rope

KNOTS USED
Gathering knot (page 19)

Cluster of 4 alternating square knots (page 30)

Square knot (page 14)

1. Cut 8 pieces of rope 100 inches (254 cm) long. Arrange all 8 cords side by side with the ends all the same length. Find the center of the group by folding the 8 cords in half all together. Cut 1 piece of rope 70 inches (178 cm) long. Tie a 4-inch (10-cm) long gathering knot around the center of the 8 cords. Trim the extra pieces of rope from the gathering knot.

2. Leave a 1¾-inch (4.5-cm) space from the gathering knot and tie 1 row of 3 decreasing alternating square knots angling toward the middle on both sides of the gathering knot. As you tie the knots, leave a ¼-inch (6-mm) gap in between each square knot. Finish the row by tying a square knot in the middle of the 16 strands of rope.

1

2

3

4

5

3. Leaving a 1½-inch (3.8-cm) space under the last row of square knots, repeat tying the decreasing alternating square knots from step 2, 4 times.

4. On both sides, with the 4 outside cords, tie 1 square knot, leaving a 3-inch (7.5-cm) space under the first square knot of the last row.

5. With the middle 8 cords, tie a cluster of 4 alternating square knots, starting 1½ inches (3.8 cm) below the row above.

6. Take the 2 outside cords on both sides of the plant hanger, and flip them while bringing them to the center of the hanger. Tie a square knot, leaving 3 inches (7.5 cm) on both sides from the previous knot.

6

7

7. With the new outside 4 cords, leaving a 2½-inch (6-cm) space below step 4, tie a square knot on both sides.

8. Cut 1 piece of rope 38 inches (96.5 cm) long. About 2½ inches (6 cm) below the knots from step 7 and 3½ inches (9 cm) below the knot from step 6, tie a gathering knot that is 1¼ inches (3 cm) wide around all the cords. The slightly different lengths will help give a bit of slack for the pot to fit.

9. Trim the cords 9 inches (23 cm) below the gathering knot.

variation

Try changing the direction of some of the square knot rows by changing the arrows from pointing down to pointing toward each other. To make this variation, start the project the same way. After tying 2 rows of decreasing alternating square knots, tie 2 rows of increasing alternating square knots with the same 1½-inch (3.8-cm) space between each row. Finish the plant hanger from step 4 onward.

8

9

VARIATION

FLORENCE PLANT HANGER

I don't know about you, but I never need a reason to add another plant to a room, and this basket plant hanger is my new favorite way to do so! I designed this project to be a cute and different take on a classic plant hanger. It's elegant in its simplicity and is a fun project to make. It looks perfect styled on its own or among a variety of different plant hangers, for an eclectic boho feel. If your style calls for a cleaner and more minimalist look, make the variation!

skill level: intermediate

MATERIALS AND TOOLS
About 110 feet (33.5 m) of 1/16-inch (1.5-mm) three-strand rope

About 54 inches (137 cm) of 1/8-inch (3-mm) three-strand rope

1 small wooden ring (ring shown has an interior diameter of 1 inch [2.5 cm])

1 metal ring, 5 inch (12.5 cm) diameter

1 metal ring, 4 inch (10 cm) diameter

KNOTS USED
Gathering knot (page 19)

Square knot (page 14)

Double half hitch (page 17)

Reverse lark's head knot (page 12)

Continuous reverse lark's head knot (page 33)

Reef knot (page 18)

Lark's head knot (page 12)

1. Using the 1/16-inch (1.5-mm) three-strand rope, cut 6 pieces 80 inches (203 cm) long. Thread the 6 pieces of rope through the wooden ring, centering the ring in the middle of the cords and leaving 40 inches (101 cm) on each side. Cut 1 piece of 1/16-inch (1.5-mm) rope 30 inches (76 cm) long. Tie a gathering knot at the bottom of the wooden ring. Trim the excess cord from the gathering knot.

2. Group the 12 strands into 3 sections, with 4 cords in each section. Tie 1 square knot with each section, 13½ inches (34 cm) down from the gathering knot.

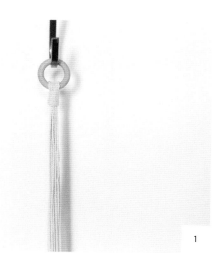

1

2

3

4

5

3. Using the ⅟₁₆-inch (1.5-mm) rope, cut 1 piece 11½ feet (3.5 m) long. Begin wrapping the 5-inch (12.5-cm) metal ring, leaving a 2-inch (5-cm) tail. After wrapping the entire ring, tie 2 double half hitches with both ends of the rope around the ring. Trim the excess rope close to the knots.

4. To attach the wrapped ring to the planter, place the working cords of the planter in front of the ring and the filler cords on the inside, right beneath each square knot. Tie a square knot right below the ring to hold it in place. Be sure to position the double half hitches in between one of the working cords to hide them.

5. Using the ⅟₁₆-inch (1.5-mm) rope, cut 12 pieces 60 inches (152 cm) long. Attach each of the 12 pieces to the wrapped ring using a reverse lark's head knot. Attach 4 of the cords, evenly spaced, within each section of the ring.

6. Begin tying 4 rows of alternating square knots using all of the cords hanging from the ring. Leave a space of about of ¾ inch (2 cm) between each row.

6

7

8

7. Using the ¹⁄₁₆-inch (1.5-mm) rope, cut 1 piece 10 feet (3 m) long. Begin wrapping the 4-inch (10-cm) metal ring, leaving a 2-inch (5-cm) tail. After wrapping the entire ring, tie 2 double half hitches with both ends of the rope. Trim the excess rope close to the knots.

8. To attach the 4-inch (10-cm) ring, repeat step 4 with each of the 12 strands.

9. Using the ¹⁄₁₆-inch (1.5-mm) rope, cut 1 piece 30 inches (76 cm) long. Tie a gathering knot using all the strands of rope as tight as possible at the bottom of the 4-inch (10-cm) ring. Trim the excess rope from the gathering knot. Cut the gathered rope at about 11½ inches (29 cm) or to your desired length. You can unravel the rope if you wish. I chose to leave mine intact.

9

10. Part A) Using the ¹⁄₁₆-inch (1.5-mm) rope, cut 2 pieces 25 inches (63.5 cm) long. Leaving a tail of 4 inches (10 cm), attach the rope to the 5-inch (12.5-cm) ring using a continuous reverse lark's head knot.

10a

10b

Part B) Attach it in 3 spots to the planter around where the cords were attached to the ring in step 4. Tie both ends together using a reef knot.

Part C) Then attach the second piece of rope to the 4-inch (10-cm) hoop, positioning the reverse lark's head knots with 3 square knots in between each section. These ropes will be used to hold the fringe. See photo on page 102 for more clarification on placement.

11. Part A) Using the ⅛-inch (3-mm) three-strand rope, cut 1 piece 27 inches (68.5 cm) long. Pull apart the rope so you are left with 3 single strands. Pull apart each of the 3 strands into 2 parts, so you are left with 6 strands.

10c

11a

Part B) Leaving a 1-inch (2.5-cm) tail, tie a lark's head knot with one of the 6 strands and attach to both of the cords you just tied on in step 10. After attaching with a lark's head knot, cut the other end at 1 inch (2.5 cm) so they are the same length. (Doing it this way is easier than precutting the small pieces and trying to attach them.) Repeat this for each of the 3 sections, filling up the whole section.

12. Trim the fringe evenly if desired, then unravel the fringe and brush with a large-tooth comb.

variation

Change the look of this plant hanger completely by skipping steps 10–12, leaving out the fringe!

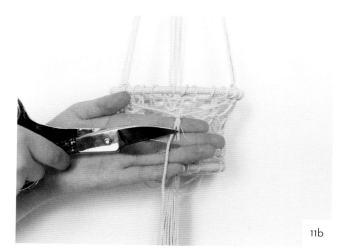

11b

12

VARIATION

SERENITY PLANT HANGER

The negative space in this plant hanger is what makes the intricate knot pattern stand out. The thin rope makes the plant hanger delicate, with a soft lace-like look. It's really versatile as it hugs a small or large pot perfectly. For a different look, you can try making this plant hanger with a larger diameter rope. Pair this plant hanger with almost any hanging plant or vary the size of the pot, because this plant hanger fits a large range of pot sizes.

skill level: advanced

MATERIALS AND TOOLS

About 169 feet (51.5 m) of ¹⁄₁₆-inch (1.5-mm) three-strand rope

1 small wooden ring (ring shown has an interior diameter of 1 inch [2.5 cm])

VARIATION

Additional 18 feet (5.5 m) of ¹⁄₁₆-inch (1.5-mm) three-strand rope

KNOTS USED

Gathering knot (page 19)

Square knot sinnet (page 22)

Square knot (page 14)

1. Cut 18 pieces of rope 110 inches (279.5 cm) long. Thread the 18 pieces of rope through the wooden ring, centering the ring in the middle of the cords and leaving 55 inches (139.5 cm) on each side. Cut 1 piece of rope 26 inches (66 cm) long. Tie a gathering knot around all of the cords at the bottom of the wood ring. Cut off the excess cord from the gathering knot.

2. Divide the 36 cords into 3 sections with 12 cords in each section. Measure 6¼ inches (16 cm) from the gathering knot and tie a square knot sinnet consisting of 3 square knots in the middle of the 12 cords. Do this with the other 2 sections.

1

2

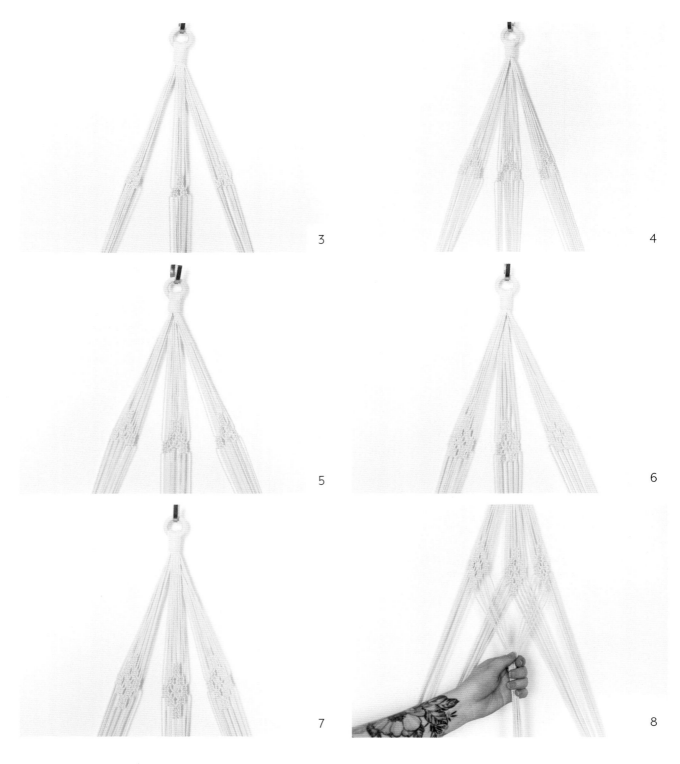

3

4

5

6

7

8

3. In all 3 sections, tie an increasing alternating square knot sinnet angling outward, leaving no space between the previous knot, consisting of 2 square knots.

4. In all 3 sections, tie an increasing alternating square knot sinnet angling outward, leaving no space between the previous knot, consisting of 3 square knots.

5. In all 3 sections, tie 1 square knot using the middle cords, positioning it ¼ inch (6 mm) below step 2's knots.

6. In all 3 sections, tie a decreasing alternating square knot sinnet going inward, leaving no space between the previous knot, consisting of 2 square knots.

7. In all 3 sections, tie a decreasing alternating square knot sinnet with the middle cords, leaving no space between the previous knot, consisting of 3 square knots.

8. Split the 3 sections of rope in half, and pair it with the section beside it. This makes 3 new sections, with 12 cords still in each section.

9. Measuring 5 inches (12.5 cm) below the last knots, repeat the same knot pattern from steps 2–7.

10. Resection the ropes by repeating step 8. Measuring 4 inches (10 cm) below the last knots and repeat the knot pattern from steps 2–7.

Cut 1 piece of rope 26 inches (66 cm) long. Around all the cords, tie a gathering knot ½ inch (1.3 cm) below the last knot. Trim the excess rope from the gathering knot.

Give the cords a final trim 12 inches (30.5 cm) below the gathering knot. If desired, unravel the cords. I left mine intact. See finished photo on page 108.

variation

Repeat the knot pattern in steps 2–7 once, 2 inches (5 cm) under the top gathering knot. Then, leaving a 1½-inch (3.8-cm) space below the last square knot sinnet, continue through the steps to complete the plant hanger. For this variation, add 10 inches (25.5 cm) of rope to each of the 18 pieces.

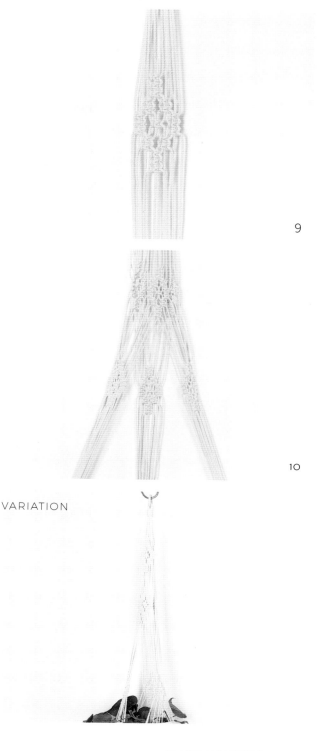

9

10

VARIATION

TERRACE PLANT HANGER

Perfectly petite, this plant hanger fits a 2-inch (5-cm) pot or a medium-size air plant and would complete any gallery wall or small space. Its unique design hangs flat against the wall, which allows you to display your plants in a fun and different way. I love this pattern for its varying linear and soft lines that accent the shapes of any plant you place in it. This intricate but approachable design is a great project to try after completing the beginner projects. Because this plant hanger is quite small, I would suggest pairing it with a plant that has smaller leaves, such as a heart-shaped philodendron, a small succulent or an air plant.

skill level: advanced

MATERIALS AND TOOLS
Approximately 85 feet (26 m) of $\frac{5}{64}$-inch (2-mm) three-strand rope

1 wooden ring, 2 inch (5 cm) diameter

KNOTS USED
Lark's head knot (page 12)

Double half hitch (page 17)

Square knot (page 14)

Gathering knot (page 19)

1. Cut 8 pieces of rope 124 inches (315 cm) long. Attach each piece to the wooden ring using a lark's head knot.

2. Tie diagonal double half hitches from the left cord to the center and then tie diagonal double half hitches from the far right cord to the center. Once you get to the center there should be an approximate gap of ½ inch (1.3 cm) between the wooden ring and the last knots.

1

2

3

4

3. Use the cord that runs through the right diagonal double half hitches to tie another double half hitch around the left cord. This will make it end in a sharp "V" shape.

4. Repeat steps 2 and 3 to complete a 2nd row of double half hitches directly beneath the row you just tied.

5. From the "V," continue tying diagonal double half hitches, angling outward to the last rope on both sides. Continue with the same angle as the row above, using the same filler cords. There should be an approximate space of 2¾ inches (7 cm) between the top of the last row and the end of this row. Repeat this step to complete a 2nd row of diagonal double half hitches directly beneath the row you just tied.

6. Tie a large square knot loosely around 10 filler cords so that all the filler cords lie flat and side by side.

5

6

7

8

7. Repeat steps 2–6 once. Then repeat steps 2–5 once. You should end with two rows of diagonal double half hitches going outward.

8. One inch (2.5 cm) below the last row, tie a cluster of 4 alternating square knots in the center of your 16 ropes. Using the first 2 cords and last 2 cords, flip the ropes and tie a square knot in front of the plant hanger 2 inches (5 cm) below the last diagonal double half hitches. This space is for your plant to sit within.

9

9. Cut a piece of rope 32 inches (81 cm) long. Tie a gathering knot 2 inches (5 cm) below both the cluster of 4 square knots and the single square knot. This 2-inch (5-cm) gap allows you to leave room for your plant. This can be hard to get the hang of at first, so to ensure your plant will fit, feel free to test it with a 2-inch (5-cm) pot before finishing your gathering knot.

10. Unravel the rope as shown on page 112 or to your desired amount. Trim the fringe to your desired length.

variation

Switch out step 6 for the beginning of step 8 to vary the look. This way you are tying a cluster of 4 alternating square knots instead of 1 large square knot. (See page 112 for image.)

10

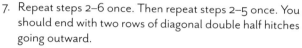

home accents

Nothing makes me more excited than gathering one-of-a-kind pieces to decorate a room. Each item has significance and value, and together they create a collection of stories and memories. Decorating a space brings me such joy, which is why I wanted to create a chapter of unique home accent pieces that I would be proud to display in my own home! I especially love the texture and boho feel of the floor pouf. My hope for your macramé table runner is that it's continually surrounded by food, love and family.

I personally feel inspired and ready to create when I'm in an environment I love, and I hope you feel the same after adding these beautiful handmade macramé pieces to your home. Because these are items that will be used around your house, be sure to spot wash them if they get stained. I love light natural cotton rope, but you may want to use darker colored rope for projects that will be in high-traffic or spill-prone areas.

AURORA PILLOW

Can you ever have enough throw pillows? Not in my opinion! My husband thinks otherwise, but that won't stop me from adding this one to my collection. Throw pillows that have different textures are some of my favorites, which is why I love the macramé pattern in this pillow. It fits perfectly in any room with any type of decor style, and I hope it becomes a favorite in your throw pillow collection as well. If you don't already have a "collection," consider this a great starting point! For this project you are making a flat panel that you will sew onto an already stuffed pillow or pillowcase. When choosing a pillow you can go with an off-white color to match the rope or have fun with a solid-colored or textured pillow, as it will slightly show through the macramé pattern and act as a background.

Note: For the whole project, tie all knots tight to each other, with no space between each row, unless otherwise stated.

skill level: beginner

MATERIALS AND TOOLS
About 300 feet (91.5 m) of ⅛-inch (3-mm) three-strand rope

Wooden dowel, ⅝ inch (1.5 cm) diameter, minimum 2 feet (61 cm) long (for temporary use only)

Needle and off-white thread

Pillow cover and pillow insert or stuffed pillow

VARIATION
Additional 130 inches (330 cm) of ⅛-inch (3-mm) three-strand rope

KNOTS USED
Lark's head knot (page 12)

Square knot (page 14)

Weave knot (page 21)

1. Cut 30 pieces of rope 120 inches (305 cm) long. Fold each piece in half and attach to the wooden dowel using a lark's head knot. (You will eventually be cutting the completed pillow off of the dowel.)

2. Leaving a gap of 2 inches (5 cm) below the dowel, complete 6 rows of alternating square knots.

1

2

3

4

5

3. On both sides, continue tying 9 rows of alternating square knots, where it is decreasing in the middle only. To do this, in each row leave out 4 cords consecutively in the middle (in your first row, 4 cords are left in the middle, then 8, then 12, then 16, and so on), until you reach 3 square knots on each side. This is the beginning of an open diamond shape.

4. With the middle 16 cords, from the start of the open diamond from step 3, tie a weave knot, working with 4 strands per working cord. Step 5 will secure the ropes in place.

5. Starting from row 11, on both sides, tie 1 row of alternating square knots in a decreasing pattern until you reach 1 square knot. Be sure to use the appropriate cords from the weave knot.

6. From row 11, repeat steps 4 and 5, once on the left side and once on the right side of the pillow. See photo for clarification.

6

7

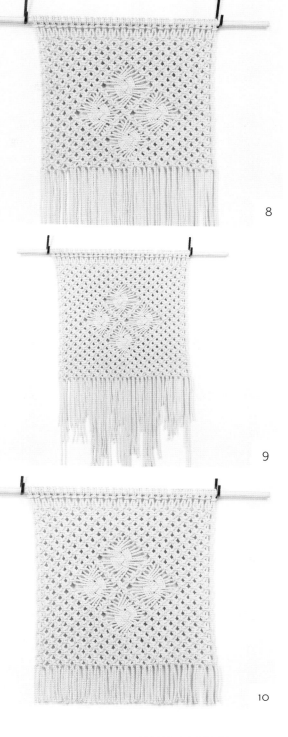

8

9

10

7. Starting from the middle in row 16, repeat steps 4 and 5.

8. On both sides, starting from the edge on row 16, continue tying increasing alternating square knots, increasing on the inside only for 10 rows.

9. From row 25, tie 4 full rows of alternating square knots. Make sure that your last row of alternating square knots are tied tight or they will undo when you unravel your ropes for the fringe.

10. Trim the extra rope at the bottom to 3½ inches (9 cm).

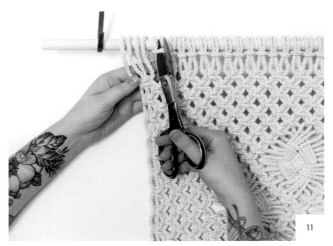

11

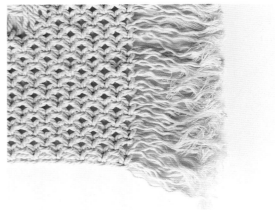

12

13

11. To cut the macramé off the dowel, cut through the middle of every lark's head knot.

12. Unravel all of the cords on both ends of the pillow and give it a final trim.

13. With a needle and thread, sew the flat panel to one side of the pillow cover or the stuffed pillow using a basic overcast or running stitch. If using a pillow cover, put the pillow insert inside the finished pillow cover and you're done!

Now the fun part, decide where you want to put it! Maybe on your couch, bed or accent chair, either individually or create another for a pair!

variation

Try tying a gathering knot in between each square knot, turning the fringe into small tassels on both sides. Cut 1 piece of ⅛-inch (3-mm) three-strand rope 130 inches (330 cm) long. Separate the rope into 3 individual pieces. Cut the 3 pieces into 30 pieces 14 inches (35.5 cm) long. Use these to tie the gathering knots beside each square knot.

VARIATION

LUMA ROPE LIGHT

This rope light is a fun and simple way to add texture and dimension to a basic light fixture. It turns a simple household item into a one-of-a-kind statement piece. I think it seamlessly fits into any decor style and looks great on its own or among a few similar pieces! You can have fun with this project by using colored rope like I did, or keep it neutral through the variation. For your convenience you can buy rope already dyed, or have fun dyeing it yourself! You can also try making this with any style sinnet.

skill level: beginner

MATERIALS AND TOOLS

About 100 feet (30.5 m) of ³⁄₁₆-inch (5-mm) three-strand black rope

About 100 feet (30.5 m) of ³⁄₁₆-inch (5-mm) three-strand natural rope

1 plug-in pendant cord light

Large-eye needle

VARIATION

100 feet (30.5 m) of ³⁄₁₆-inch (5-mm) three-strand natural rope (instead of 100 feet [30.5 m] of black rope)

KNOTS USED

Overhand knot (page 18)

Double half knot sinnet (page 25)

1. Cut 1 piece of each rope 100 feet (30.5 m) long. The black cord will be cord A, and the white will be cord B and the light's electrical cord will act as the filler cord. Attach cord A to the base of the light fixture by tying it to the electrical cord with an overhand knot; repeat with cord B under cord A. Bundle the cords for convenience, if needed (page 42).

2. Move cord B's working cords out of the way by placing them behind and tie a left-facing half knot around the electrical cord with cord A.

3

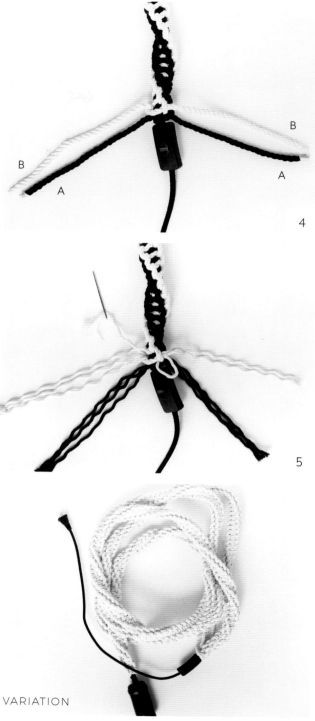

4

5

3. Repeat step 2 with cord B now, moving cord A out the way to tie a left-facing half knot with cord B.

4. Repeat steps 2 and 3 until you reach your desired length or have covered all of the light's cord. Make sure to keep your knots tight and push up on them after every 5 or so knots if you need to, so that the electrical cord doesn't show through.

5. To finish your sinnet, cut all 4 strands of remaining rope to about 7 inches (18 cm). Unravel the ends of each piece of rope. Using a large-eye needle, sew the ends back into the sinnet. Cut the excess pieces close to the sinnet so you don't see them.

variation
Change the look of this pendant light completely by using the same colored rope for a subtle, tone-on-tone look!

VARIATION

RILEY'S RUG

I am in love with this rug and honestly, my cats might even be bigger fans! I named this project after my cat Riley, who did not want to stop lying on it! It's the perfect size for an entryway rug or can be used as a small accent rug for any room. A lot of the projects in this book are hung on the wall, so it was fun to create something for a different part of the house. Floors need some love, too! The texture of this rug really feels great under your feet, so I hope that you (and your pets) love it as much as we do.

Note: Tie all knots tight to each other, with no space between each row, unless otherwise stated.

skill level: intermediate

MATERIALS AND TOOLS
About 477 feet (145 m) of ³⁄₁₆-inch (5-mm) three-strand rope

Wooden dowel, minimum 2 feet (61 cm) long (for temporary use only)

VARIATION
130 inches (330 cm) of ³⁄₁₆-inch (5-mm) three-strand rope

KNOTS USED
Lark's head knot (page 12)

Square knot (page 14)

Weave knot (page 21)

Reef knot (page 18, for variation)

1. Cut 26 pieces of rope 18 feet 4 inches (5.5 m) long. Fold each piece in half and attach it with a lark's head knot to the wooden dowel. Bundle the ropes if needed for convenience (see page 42). (You will eventually be cutting the completed rug off of the dowel.)

2. Leave a gap of ¾ inch (2 cm) from the dowel and then complete 2 rows of alternating square knots.

1

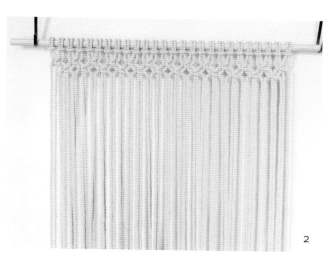

2

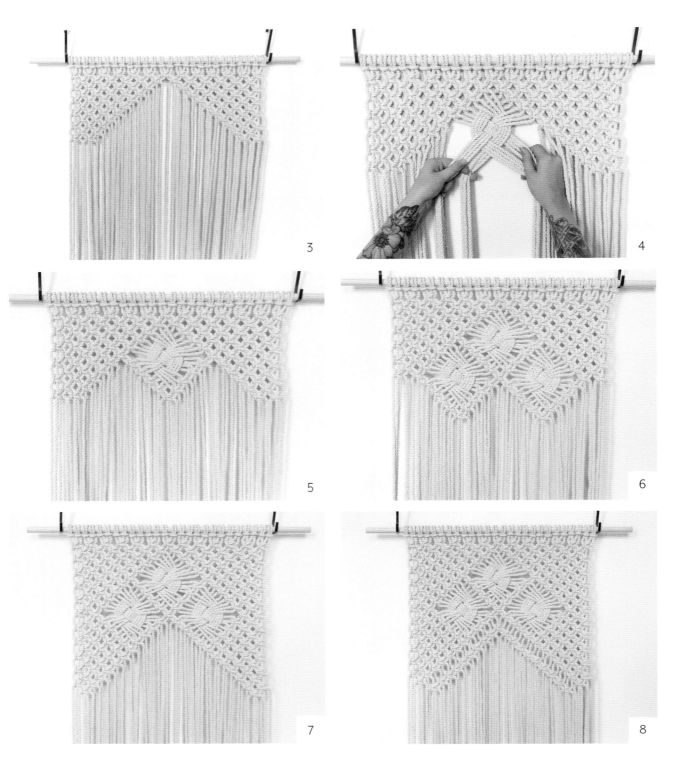

3. Continue tying 9 rows of decreasing alternating square knots, where it is decreasing in the middle only; the edges will stay straight for the edge of the rug. To do this, leave out 4 cords consecutively in the middle of each row (in your first row, 4 cords are left in the middle, then 8, then 12, then 16 and so on), until you reach 2 square knots on each side and 36 ropes in the middle. This is the beginning of a diamond shape.

4. With the middle 16 cords, from the start of the open diamond from step 3, tie a weave knot, working with 4 stands per working cord. The next step will secure the ropes.

5. Starting from row 6, on both sides, tie 1 row of 5 decreasing alternating square knots, angling inward. Make sure to use the appropriate cords from the weave knot.

6. From row 7 repeat steps 4 and 5, once on the left side and once on the right side in the open diamonds. See photo for clarification.

7. On both sides of the rug, tie increasing alternating square knots (increasing on the inside of the rug only) from rows 11–17. From rows 17–22, tie decreasing alternating square knots on either side (decreasing on the inside of the rug only). See photo for clarification.

8. Starting from the middle in row 11, leave a 1-inch (2.5-cm) space and tie 1 row of 10 alternating square knots on the left side. Tie 1 row of 9 alternating square knots on the right side, leaving the same consistent 1-inch (2.5-cm) gap.

9. With the middle 32 ropes, tie a weave knot, using 8 strands as each working cord. The next step will secure the ropes.

10. Starting from row 22, on both sides, tie 1 row of alternating square knots in a decreasing pattern, using the appropriate strands from the weave knot, until you reach 1 square knot.

11. On both sides, from rows 22–28, tie increasing alternating square knots, leaving a 1-inch (2.5-cm) gap between the knots you are tying next to the middle section. See photo for clarification.

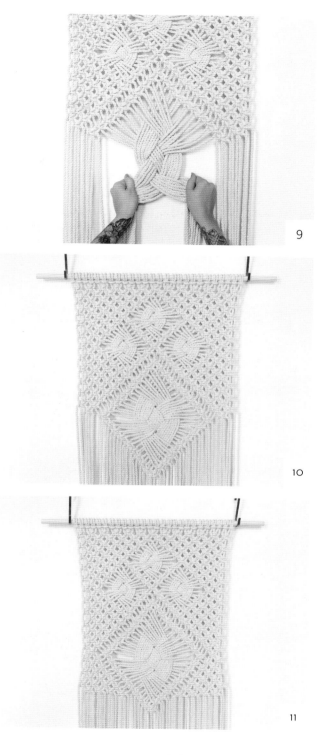

9

10

11

12

13

14

15

12. On both sides, tie decreasing alternating square knots from rows 28–33 (decreasing only on the inside of the rug).

13. On both sides, starting from row 28, tie 1 row of 5 decreasing alternating square knots, angling inward, leaving a 1-inch (2.5-cm) gap between the knots you tied in the middle section.

14. On both sides, using the middle 16 cords within the start of the open diamonds, tie a weave knot, using 4 stands per working cord. On both sides, starting from row 34, tie 1 row of decreasing alternating square knots, using the appropriate strands from the weave knot, until you reach 1 square knot in row 39.

15. From row 34, with the middle 16 cords, tie a weave knot, using 4 stands per working cord on both sides. On both sides, starting from row 38, tie 1 row of decreasing alternating square knots, using the appropriate strands from the weave knot, until you reach 1 square knot.

16

17

16. Starting back at row 33, tie increasing alternating square knots on both sides until you reach row 43. You should end with a flat base.

17. Trim the extra rope at the bottom to approximately 3 inches (7.5 cm).

18. To cut off the rug from the dowel, cut through the middle of every lark's head knot. (See Aurora Pillow step 11 photo, page 122, for clarification.)

   Unravel the entire fringe on both ends of the rug and give it a final trim.

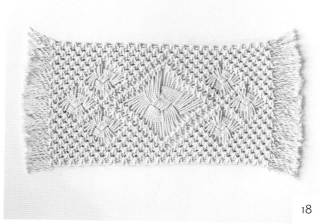

18

 variation

Try tying a simple reef knot around the fringe beside each square knot, turning the full fringe into small tassels. Position the reef knot on the back of the rug. Using ³⁄₁₆-inch (5-mm) three-strand rope, cut 1 piece of rope 130 inches (330 cm) long. Separate the rope into 3 individual strands. Cut each strand into 28 pieces approximately 10 inches (25.5 cm) long. Use these to tie the reef knots. Trim the fringe again if needed.

VARIATION

ASPEN HANGING SHELF

It's a great feeling making something both practical and beautiful, and I think this shelf combines both of those traits flawlessly. This shelf is another way to bring macramé into your home in a unique and useful way. The striking geometric design and soft macramé details come together to create an interesting piece that I hope you'll love using to show off some of your favorite items. As soon as it went up in my house, I immediately started getting requests to make them from friends and family, so brace yourself for that very real possibility!

skill level: intermediate

MATERIALS AND TOOLS
Drill and ½-inch (12-mm) drill bit

Sandpaper

6 feet (183 cm) of ¹⁄₁₆-inch (1.5-mm) three-strand rope

About 272 feet (83 m) of ⁵⁄₆₄-inch (2-mm) three-strand rope

1 metal ring, 3 inch (7.5 cm) diameter

Shelf 1 wood dimensions: 17¾ x 7¼ x ¾ inch (45 x 18.5 x 2 cm)

Shelf 2 wood dimensions: 24 x 7¼ x ¾ inches (61 x 18.5 x 2 cm)

KNOTS USED
Double half hitch (page 17)

Gathering knot (page 19)

Square knot (page 14)

PREPPING THE WOOD SHELVES
I used unstained ash wood for my shelves, but any type of wood will work. You can stain, paint or clear coat the wood before making the project. Make sure your wood is cut to the right dimensions. Most lumber stores will cut wood for you if you don't have a saw.

Mark where you will drill the holes by referring to the diagram.

Using a ½-inch (12-mm) drill bit, drill through the wood in the 8 places marked on each piece of wood. Sand the edges of the shelf and around the drilled holes.

ASPEN SHELF MEASUREMENTS

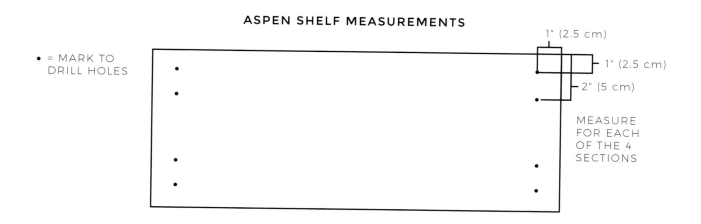

- = MARK TO DRILL HOLES

1" (2.5 cm)

1" (2.5 cm)

2" (5 cm)

MEASURE FOR EACH OF THE 4 SECTIONS

1

2

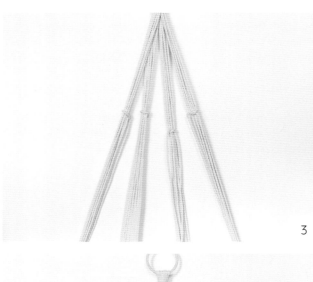

3

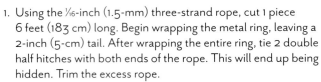

4

1. Using the 1/16-inch (1.5-mm) three-strand rope, cut 1 piece 6 feet (183 cm) long. Begin wrapping the metal ring, leaving a 2-inch (5-cm) tail. After wrapping the entire ring, tie 2 double half hitches with both ends of the rope. This will end up being hidden. Trim the excess rope.

2. Using the 5/64-inch (2-mm) three-strand rope, cut 16 pieces 16 feet (4.87 m) long. Place the 16 strands through the wrapped ring, centering them (with 8 feet [2.44 m] on each side of the ring). Be sure to cover the double half hitches with the 16 strands. Using the 5/64-inch (2-mm) three-strand rope, cut 1 piece 36 inches (91 cm) long. Tie a 1-inch (2.5-cm) gathering knot around the 32 strands right below the wrapped ring. Trim the excess rope from the gathering knot.

3. Evenly divide the 32 strands of rope into 4 sections, with 8 cords in each section. When you are dividing the cords, make sure to section the pieces with other pieces that are naturally positioned beside each other for a cleaner look. These will become the 4 straps (2 front straps and 2 back straps). I tied a loose knot around each section simply to highlight them, but it's not necessary. When working with each section, the cords should be free.

4. Position 2 of the sections that are across from each other to become the front straps, and position the other 2 sections as the back straps. Do the following for both back straps: Use the middle 4 cords and tie 1 square knot right under the gathering knot. Continue to tie a total of 40 rows of alternating square knots, ending with 2 square knots.

5

6

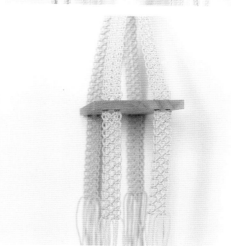

7

5. For each of the front straps, do the following: Use the middle 4 cords and tie 1 square knot right under the gathering knot. Continue to tie a total of 42 rows of alternating square knots, ending with 2 square knots.

6. Take shelf 1 and thread the 4 strands through each corresponding hole. Once all 4 sections have been threaded through, tie 1 square knot with each of the 2 groups of 4 strands in each of the 4 sections, directly under the wooden shelf.

7. In all 4 sections, tie a total of 25 rows of alternating square knots ending with 2 square knots.

8. Repeat step 6 with shelf 2. Then tie 1 alternating square knot beneath the 2 square knots.

8

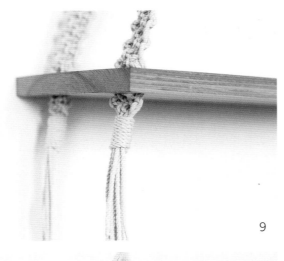

9. Using the 5/64-inch (2-mm) three-strand rope, cut 4 pieces 38 inches (96.5 cm) long. Tie 4 gathering knots 1 inch (2.5 cm) wide with all the cords under the square knot from step 8. Trim the excess cord from the gathering knot.

10. Trim the extra rope at the bottom of the 4 tassels to about 11½ inches (29 cm), or to your desired length. Unravel all of the ropes and give it a final trim if needed.

When hanging, position the shelf so that the back shorter straps are the ones against the wall. This will keep the shelf flush to the wall and level. I designed this shelf so it hangs flat to the wall. If you want it to be free floating, make the front and back straps the same length in steps 4 and 5.

9

variation

Make yourself a single shelf by leaving out steps 7 and 8 and finishing the same way from step 9 forward. Cut 16 pieces of 5/64-inch (2-mm) three-strand rope to 11 feet (3.35 m cm) instead of the lengths listed in step 1.

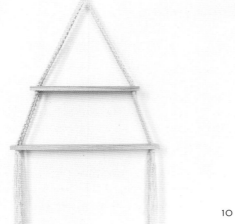

10

VARIATION

BOHO FLOOR POUF

Who doesn't love a cute floor pouf, especially one that you can make yourself?! This boho beauty is a unique piece that I designed to make macramé a part of a home's essential furniture. With so many macramé projects created to be pieces of art on the wall, it's nice to make something with utility that you can physically enjoy and rest your feet on. This project will take a lot of time and patience to complete, but I know that I'm always so much more satisfied when I spend more time on something! The finished pouf will be about 20 inches (51 cm) wide by 12 inches (30.5 cm) tall.

Note: Unless otherwise stated, tie all knots and rows tight together.

skill level: advanced

MATERIALS AND TOOLS

About 1,190 feet (362.7 m) of ³⁄₁₆-inch (5-mm) three-strand rope

¾-inch (2-cm) wooden dowel, 60 inches (152 cm) long (for temporary use only)

Large-eye needle

3 foam cushions, 3 x 18 x 18 inches (7.5 cm x 45 cm x 45 cm)

Quilt batting

VARIATION

Additional 200 inches (508 cm) of ³⁄₁₆-inch (5-mm) three-strand rope

KNOTS USED

Lark's head knot (page 12)

Double half hitch (page 19)

Half knot (page 13)

Reef knot (page 18)

SIDE PANEL

1. Cut 60 pieces of rope 140 inches (356 cm) long. Attach all 60 pieces of rope to the temporary dowel using a lark's head knot.

2. Cut 2 pieces of rope 60 inches (152 cm) long. Leaving a space of 3 inches (7.5 cm) from the dowel, tie a row of double half hitches with all 120 pieces of rope, using one of the 60 inch (152 cm) ropes as the filler cord. Set the other 60 inch (152 cm) rope aside.

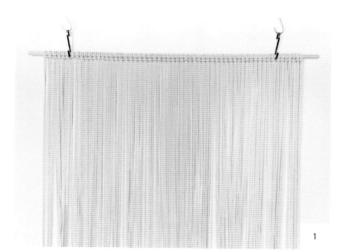

1

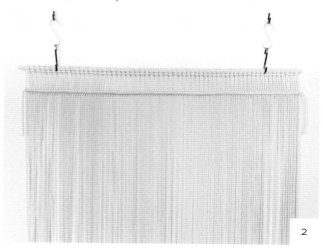

2

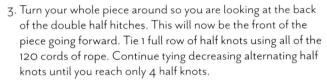

3

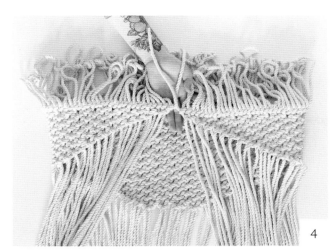

4

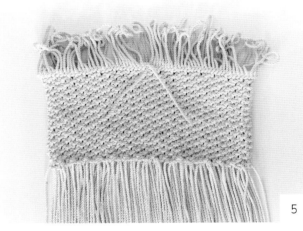

5

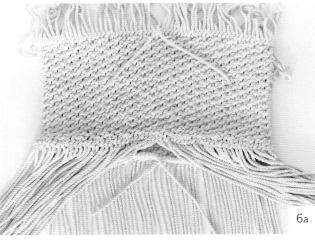

6a

3. Turn your whole piece around so you are looking at the back of the double half hitches. This will now be the front of the piece going forward. Tie 1 full row of half knots using all of the 120 cords of rope. Continue tying decreasing alternating half knots until you reach only 4 half knots.

4. Now slide the whole piece off of the dowel, placing the front of the piece on the floor, and fold both ends toward the middle. Refer to photo for help with placement (shown where my hand is).

5. Starting from the 2nd row of alternating half knots, continue tying rows of increasing alternating half knots until you reach the last 4 half knots from step 2. Working in the round like this avoids having to sew together a seam.

6. Part A) Using the other 60-inch (152-cm) cord you cut in step 2, and working from the inside and around the bottom, tie a row of double half hitches with all 120 cords, until you reach your first knot. This photo shows the whole row complete. Refer to 6B for further clarification.

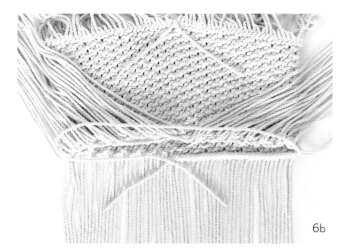

6b

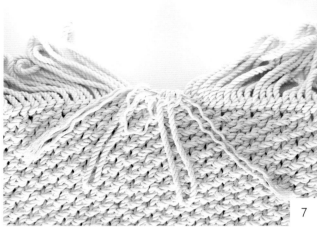

7

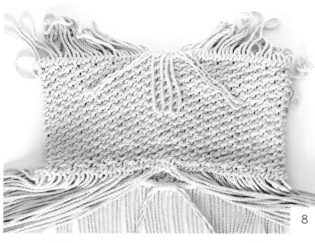

8

9

6. Part B) Make sure you are tying the double half hitches from the inside, so the backs of the double half hitches become a part of the front circular side panel. This photo shows a quarter of the row complete.

7. Where there is a gap between the first and last knot in the row of double half hitches, unravel the filler cords coming out from the knot. Using a large-eye needle sew the unraveled pieces into at least 2 knots of double half hitches on both sides. Complete this for the top and bottom.

8. Pull both ends from both rows of double half hitches tight together, so there is no space in between the knots. This will make it look like a seamless row of double half hitches. Put this panel aside to use later.

TOP AND BOTTOM PANELS

9. Cut 8 pieces of rope 96 inches (244 cm) long and 16 pieces 132 inches (335 cm) long. Attach all the ropes to the temporary dowel using a lark's head knot, with the longest cords in the middle and 4 of the shorter pieces on either side.

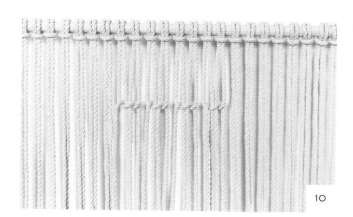

10. Leaving a 3-inch (7.5-cm) gap from the dowel, tie 4 half knots with the middle 16 cords.

11. Continue tying increasing alternating half knots for 4 rows.

12. Tie 2 rows of alternating half knots, and then 1 row of increasing alternating half knots.

13. Repeat step 12, until you reach the last ropes on either side at both edges of the panel.

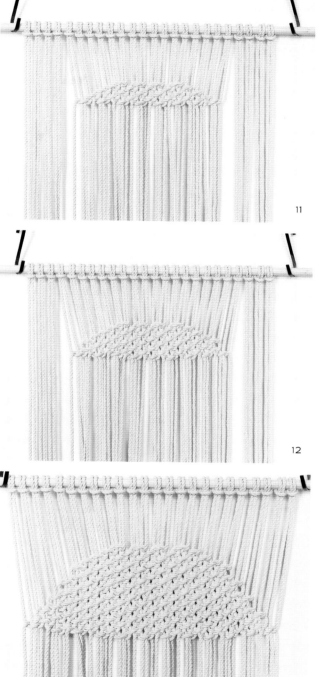

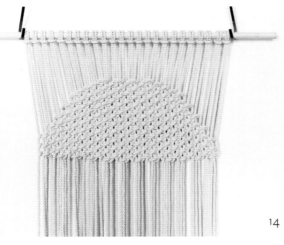

14

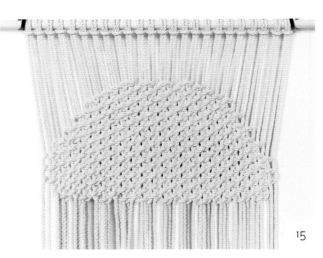

15

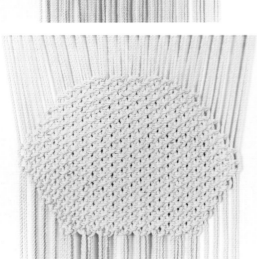

16

14. Tie 2 more rows of alternating half knots.

15. Tie 2 rows of decreasing half knots and 1 row of alternating half knots.

16. Repeat step 15 until you reach 12 half knots.

17. Tie 5 rows of decreasing alternating half knots, ending in 4 half knots.

17

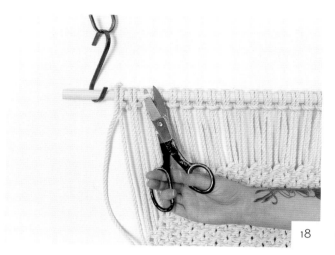

18

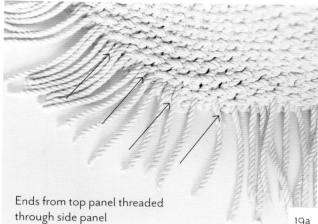

Ends from top panel threaded
through side panel

19a

18. Cut the panel off the dowel by cutting in between each of
the lark's head knots.

Make another panel following steps 9–18. One will be the
top panel, and the other panel will be the bottom.

ASSEMBLING THE FLOOR POUF

19. Situating one of the top/bottom panels on the floor, take
the round side panel, place it on top and line up the edges.
Thread the ends through the side panel, just under the
double half hitch. Your taped ends will make it easy to do,
but feel free to use a large-eye needle if you find it easier. Do
this to each one of the cords from the top panel. It is okay
that the cords are loose for now, as they will be secured with
knots later.

20. Trace and cut out a 16-inch (40.5-cm) circle out of all
3 of the foam cushions. Fold the batting into a square so
there are 4 layers that are 16 inches (40.5 cm) wide. Cut
a 16-inch (40.5-cm) circle out of the 4 layers of folded
batting. Fold a new piece of the batting in half so it is 10 to
12 inches (25.5 to 30.5 cm) wide. Cut it so that you have
one two-layer piece of batting that's 57 inches (145 cm)
long.

With the top and side panel loosely attached, place the
16-inch (40.5-cm) circle of batting inside the upside-down
pouf.

19b

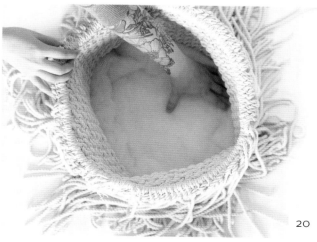

20

21

22

23

24

21. Take the 57-inch (145-cm) folded piece of batting and wrap it around the 3 pieces of foam cushioning stacked on top of each other.

22. Place the 3 cushions wrapped in batting inside the side panel. Adjust the batting and foam so they are lying relatively flat. There will be approximately a ½-inch (1.3-cm) gap between the base of the foam cushion and the bottom double half hitch from the side panel. Feel free to line the batting around the inside of the walls of the pouf first and then place each foam cushion in one at a time if it is easier for you.

23. Carefully flip over the loosely attached side and top panel. With the first half of a reef knot, tightly tie together the two side-by-side pieces of rope that have been threaded through from step 19. Continue this all the way around the pouf so there are no cords left. Refer to the photo for clarification.

24. Flip the pouf over so you are looking at the open base. Similarly to step 19, thread the bottom panel cords through the side panel beside the double half hitch. Tie half of a tight reef knot. Do this to every cord so all the cords have been tied and accounted for.

25a

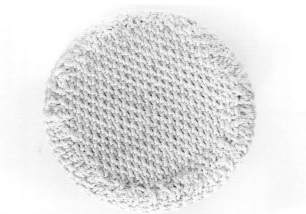

Base of pouf with ends sewn in 25b

25. Trim all cords to 4 or 5 inches (10 or 12.5 cm) so they are easier to work with. Unravel one cord at a time and, using a large-eye needle, sew the 3 unraveled pieces into the panels. Trim the cord close to the pouf and push the end into the fabric of the pouf (this helps hide the ends). Do this to each one of the cords, so there are no cords remaining.

26. Flip the floor pouf back over so it's sitting on the base. Trim the cords to about 3 inches (7.5 cm), or your desired length, and unravel all of the cords at the top for the fringe; trim again if desired.

You're finally done! Now find where you want to put it, kick up your feet and enjoy all of your hard work!

26

Try making tassels with the fringe by gathering the same size small section all the way around and tying a reef knot around each section. Using ³⁄₁₆-inch (5-mm) three-strand rope, cut 1 piece of rope 200 inches (508 cm) long. Cut that into 20 pieces 10 inches (25.4 cm) long. Separate the ropes into 3 individual strands. With each piece, tie a reef knot around a small section of tassel. Position the reef knot at the back of each tassel so you don't see it from the front. After completing 1 row of reef knots, split each tassel in half and tie a reef knot around both new sections using the same amount of rope. This creates an alternating tassel pattern.

VARIATION

HEIRLOOM TABLE RUNNER

This project is a unique way to bring macramé into your dining room. It looks incredible draped across a table and can stand alone for everyday use or be part of a beautiful tablescape for special occasions. The table is such an important part of a home, and I wanted to create a project that brought macramé into that space so that it could become a part of your family's shared memories. This project will finish at roughly 7 feet (213 cm) long.

Note: When tying the knots on each angle, follow the same angle as the row above it.

skill level: advanced

MATERIALS AND TOOLS

About 565 feet (172.2 m) of ⁵⁄₆₄-inch (2-mm) three-strand rope

Wooden dowel, minimum 12 inches (30.5 cm) long (for temporary use only)

KNOTS USED

Lark's head knot (page 12)

Square knot (page 14)

Double half hitch (page 17)

Variation: Overhand knot (page 18)

1. Cut 20 pieces of rope 28¼ feet (8.6 m) long. Attach all 20 pieces of rope to the dowel using a lark's head knot (you will cut the runner off the dowel later).

2. Leaving an 11-inch (28-cm) space, tie 1 square knot in the very middle of the 20 cords. Next, tie 2 increasing alternating square knots tight to the single square knot above.

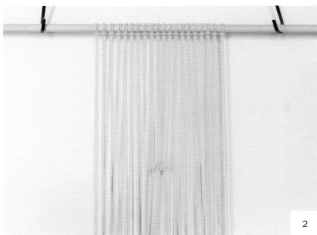

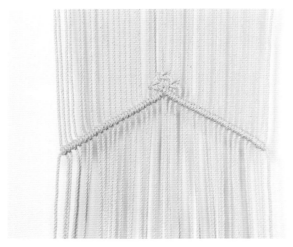

3

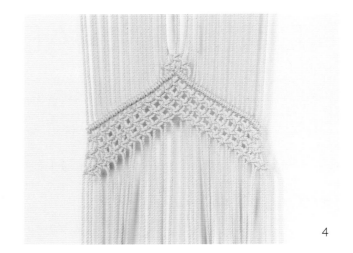

4

5

3. Under the 3 square knots, use the middle 2 cords and tie 20 diagonal double half hitches angling out to the right. Using the first cord from the first double half hitch, tie 19 diagonal double half hitches angling out to the left.

4. Tie 3 tight rows of increasing alternating square knots to the edge of the runner on both sides (consisting of 10 square knots in each row).

5. Tie a diagonal double half hitch angling out to the right. Using the cord from the first double half hitch, tie a diagonal double half hitch angling out to the left. Tie both rows tight to the square knots above it.

6. Leaving a space of 3 inches (7.5 cm) in the center, tie 1 row of 4 increasing alternating square knots on both sides.

6

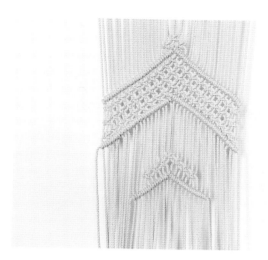

7

8

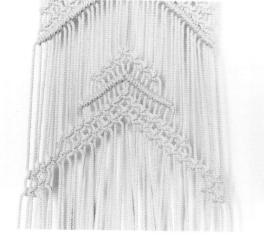

9

7. Leaving a ½-inch (1.3-cm) space, tie 10 diagonal double half hitches angling out to the right. Using the cord from the first double half hitch, tie 9 diagonal double half hitches angling out to the left.

8. Leaving a ½-inch (1.3-cm) space from the row above, tie 1 row of 7 increasing alternating square knots angling out on both sides. Tight to the previous row, tie 1 row of 10 increasing alternating square knots angling out on both sides.

9. On both sides, starting 2 cords in, tie a row of 2 increasing alternating square knots tight to the row above it.

10. Leaving a 2-inch (5-cm) space from the row above, tie 14 diagonal double half hitches angling out to the right. Using the cord from the first double half hitch, tie 13 diagonal double half hitches angling out to the left. In the middle of the double half hitches, leave a space of ½ inch (1.3 cm) and tie 1 row of 5 increasing alternating square knots angling out on each side. In the middle of the alternating square knots, tie 1 square knot using 1 working cord and 8 filler cords.

10

11

12

13

11. Starting under the square knots from step 10, tie 1 row of 4 decreasing alternating square knots using the corresponding cords from the previous step, angling inward (make sure not to overlap the cords).

12. Continuing the diamond of double half hitches from step 10 (using the same filler cord), tie 13 diagonal double half hitches angling in from the right and 14 angling in from the left. Continue to leave the same ½-inch (1.3-cm) space when tying the row.

13. On both sides, leaving a 1¾-inch (4.5-cm) space from the square knot from step 9, tie 1 row of 5 increasing alternating square knots angling in and 1 row of 4 decreasing alternating square knots angling out.

    Continuing the same angle, from the double half hitch row from step 12, tie 16 diagonal double half hitches angling out to the right. Using the cord from the first double half hitch, tie 15 diagonal double half hitches angling out to the left.

14. Leaving a ½-inch (1.3-cm) space below the double half hitches, tie 2 rows of increasing alternating square knots with 6 square knots in the 1st row and 4 square knots in the 2nd row.

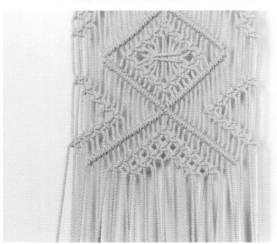

14

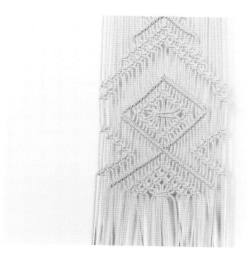

15

16

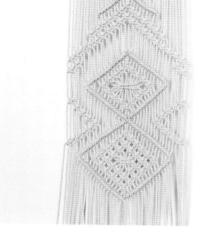

17

15. Within the alternating square knots, tie 1 large square knot using 1 working cord and 6 filler cords.

16. Finish the diamond by tying 2 rows of decreasing alternating square knots with 3 square knots in the 1st row and 4 in the 2nd row.

17. Continuing the diamond (using the same filler cord) of double half hitches from step 13, tie 15 diagonal double half hitches angling in on the right and 16 angling in on the left. Continue to leave the same ½-inch (1.3-cm) space between the previous row in step 14.

18. Leaving a 2-inch (5-cm) space between the square knot from step 13, repeat the first part of step 13.

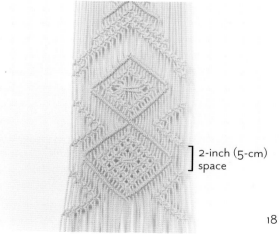

2-inch (5-cm) space

18

19

20

21

19. Continuing the same angle from the double half hitch row from step 17, tie 20 diagonal double half hitches angling out to the right. Using the cord from the first double half hitch, tie 19 diagonal double half hitches angling out to the left at the edge of the runner on both sides.

    Leaving a ¾-inch (2-cm) space under the previous row, tie 2 rows of 10 increasing alternating square knots. Tight to the row above, tie 15 diagonal double half hitches angling out to the right. Using the cord from the first double half hitch, tie 14 diagonal double half hitches angling out to the left.

20. In the center of the double half hitches you just tied, tie 1 large square knot using 2 working cords and 18 filler cords.

21. Continuing the diamond of double half hitches from the first part of step 19 (using the same filler cords), tie 14 double half hitches angling in from the right and 15 angling in from the left. Be sure to use the corresponding cords from the large square knot and be careful not to crisscross any cords.

22. Continue through the steps in reverse, as the runner is symmetrical. When going through the steps, be sure to always angle inward instead of outward and vise versa. Start from the second part of step 19 (the rows of square knots) and work your way backward.

22

23

23. After completing all the steps in reverse, cut the cords at 11 inches (28 cm) following the angle of the last rows.

24. Cut the table runner off of the dowel by cutting in between each of the lark's head knots.

25. Cut the ropes on the side you just cut off the dowel at the same 11-inch (28-cm) angle as the rows below it, matching the cut you made in step 23. Unravel all of the cords and trim again if desired.

You're finished! Now drape it over your table and enjoy your hard work!

variation

Try changing how the fringe looks by tying an overhand knot, with each cord, 1 inch (2.5 cm) in from the ends before unraveling the rope. After tying the overhand knots all the way across on both sides, unravel the rope after the overhand knot.

24

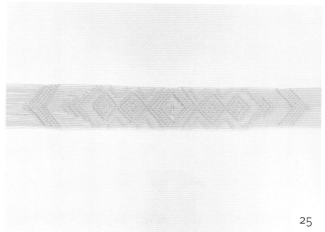

25

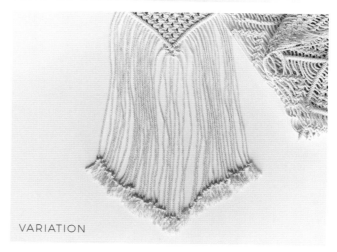

VARIATION

ETHERIA LANTERN

This project is awesome because it can be many things—a lantern, a mobile or a three-dimensional art piece. It's truly a dramatic statement piece and a unique addition to any room or outdoor space. Its open and complex details add visual interest and varying texture to the space it's a part of. You can hang a bulb through the center opening to easily make it a functioning lantern, or enjoy it on its own!

skill level: advanced

MATERIALS AND TOOLS

About 506 feet (154 m) of $\frac{5}{64}$-inch (2-mm) three-strand rope

About 111 inches (282 cm) of $\frac{3}{16}$-inch (5-mm) three-strand rope

1 wooden ring, 2 inches (5 cm) diameter

2 metal rings, 1½ inches (3.8 cm) diameter

1 embroidery hoop, 8 inches (20 cm) diameter (inside hoop only)

2 embroidery hoops, 10 inches (25.5 cm) diameter (inside hoop only)

1 embroidery hoop, 6 inches (15 cm) diameter (inside hoop only)

Large-tooth comb

KNOTS USED

Gathering knot (page 19)

Double half hitch (page 17)

Square knot (page 14)

Reverse lark's head knot (page 12)

Continuous reverse lark's head knot (page 33)

Reef knot (page 18)

Lark's head knot (page 12)

Project note: I used secondhand embroidery hoops from a thrift store on my final project photo. My 2-inch (5-cm) wooden ring was much lighter in color than the older, worn, embroidery hoops. To darken the wood ring, I dyed it with black tea. If you have a similar situation, simply boil water and make a cup of black tea. Remove the tea bag after letting it steep for 5 minutes. Submerge the wooden ring in the tea for 5 minutes, then take it out and let it dry.

1

2

3

1. Using ⅚₄-inch (2-mm) three-strand rope, cut 8 pieces 134 feet (40.8 m) long. Thread the 8 pieces through the wooden ring, centering the cords so there are 67 feet (20 m) on either side. Using ⅚₄-inch (2-mm) three-strand rope, cut 1 piece 22 inches (55.8 cm) long. Using that cord, tie a gathering knot 1 inch (2.5 cm) wide around the 16 cords, right below the wooden ring.

2. With one of the 1½-inch (3.8-cm) metal rings, thread all of the cords through it and position it 3½ inches (9 cm) below the gathering knot. Tie a double half hitch around the ring with each cord.

3. Tie 4 square knots tight to the previous row. Tie 2 tight rows of alternating square knots and then repeat step 2 to attach the second metal ring.

4. Attach the 8-inch (20-cm) embroidery hoop (inside hoop only) by tying a double half hitch around the hoop 6½ inches (16.5 cm) below the last ring with each of the 16 cords, spacing the cords by referring to the diagram on the next page.

4

ETHERIA LANTERN ROPE PLACEMENT FOR STEP #4

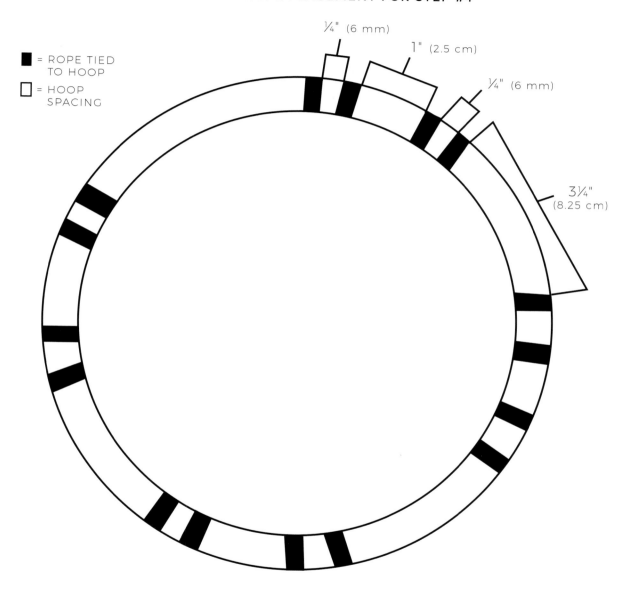

¼" (6 mm)

1" (2.5 cm)

¼" (6 mm)

3¼" (8.25 cm)

■ = ROPE TIED TO HOOP

□ = HOOP SPACING

5

6

7

5. Using ⁵⁄₆₄-inch (2-mm) three-strand rope, cut 24 pieces of rope 111 inches (282 cm) long. Fold the cords in half and attach each with a reverse lark's head knot. Do this in each of the 4 sections, working from left to right: add 1 cord to the left of the already attached cords, 1 cord in the ¼-inch (6-mm) space, 2 cords in the 1-inch (2.5-cm) space, 1 cord in the ¼-inch (6-mm) space and 1 cord on the right side of the already attached cord.

6. In each of the 4 sections, use the first left cord as the filler cord and tie horizontal double half hitches tight to the reverse lark's head knot.

7. In each of the 4 sections, tie 4 square knots right under the double half hitches. Continue tying 3 rows of decreasing alternating square knots, ending with 1 square knot.

8. Working in between the 4 sections, take the 2 outer cords from each side and tie a square knot 2 inches (5 cm) below the embroidery hoop. Continue tying 2 rows of alternating square knots with the next 4 cords in line under the first 2. Leave a 1-inch (2.5-cm) gap between each row of square knots.

8

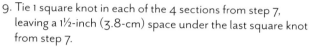

9

10

9. Tie 1 square knot in each of the 4 sections from step 7, leaving a 1½-inch (3.8-cm) space under the last square knot from step 7.

10. Tie 2 rows of alternating square knots with all of the cords all the way around the hoop, leaving the same 1-inch (2.5-cm) spacing between each row.

11. Using the 10-inch (25.5-cm) embroidery hoop (inside hoop only), take the filler cord from each square knot and place them on the outside of the hoop. Then place the working cords on the inside. Alternating the knots from the row above, tie 1 square knot loosely to the hoop all the way around the hoop.

12. Using $\frac{5}{64}$-inch (2-mm) three-strand rope, cut 32 pieces 72 inches (183 cm) long. Fold each rope in half and, using a reverse lark's head knot, attach 2 cords to the wood hoop in between the middle of the filler cords from each square knot from step 11. Continue this all the way around the hoop.

11

12

13

14

15

13. Tie 1 square knot with each of the newly added 4 cords, tight to the wood hoop.

14. Tie 1 full row of alternating square knots all the way around the hoop, leaving no space between the rows.

15. For this row, tie 1 alternating square knot, then skip 4 cords and tie another alternating square knot. Continue this pattern all the way around the hoop, leaving no space between the rows.

16. In the open space, tie 1 large square knot using 1 working cord and 6 filler cords; continue this on every other space, leaving 8 cords in between each section.

16

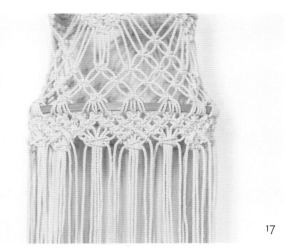

17

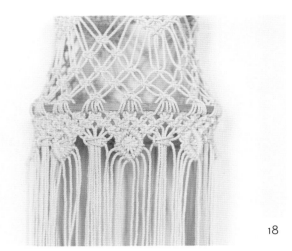

18

17. In the open space left from step 16, tie the top half of a
    double half hitch diamond, tight to the square knots above.
    In the middle of what will be a diamond, tie 1 large square
    knot using 1 working cord and 4 filler cords.

18. Continue the bottom half of the double half hitch diamond
    using the same filler cord from the bottom double half
    hitches, angling inward, ending with a point.

19. Tie 1 square knot under the single square knot from step
    15 using the corresponding cord from the double half
    hitches and large square knots from step 16.

20. Tie 2 full rows of alternating square knots all the way
    around the hoop, leaving no space between the rows.

19

20

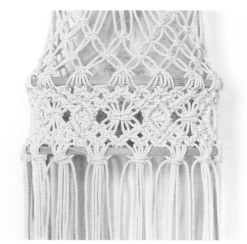

21

22

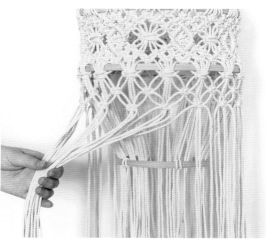

23

24

21. Using the remaining 10-inch (25.5-cm) embroidery hoop (inside hoop only), take every other square knot and place all the cords from the square knot on the outside of the hoop. With the other square knots, take the filler cord from each square knot and place them on the inside of the hoop, and place the working cords on the outside. Use the filler cords from the square knots on the inside of the hoop and tie 1 large alternating square knot using 1 working cord around 6 filler cords from the cords on the outside of the hoop. Do this all the way around the hoop.

22. With the working cords and outer filler cords of the large square knots from step 21, tie 2 rows of alternating square knots, leaving a 1-inch (2.5-cm) space between each row. There should be a total of 16 square knots in each row.

23. Of the 6 filler cords from the previous step, take 4 of the middle filler cords and place them inside the 6-inch (15-cm) wood hoop while holding it. Taking 4 cords from the inside of the hoop, hold the 6-inch (15-cm) hoop 6 inches (15 cm) below the 10-inch (25.5-cm) wood hoop. Tie a double half hitch with each of the 4 cords around the 6-inch (15-cm) hoop. When choosing which 4 cords to use, choose them in a 12, 3, 6 and 9 o'clock pattern. Take the remaining filler cords from step 21 and place them freely hanging inside the 6-inch (15-cm) hoop.

24. Using ³⁄₁₆-inch (5-mm) three-strand rope, cut 24 pieces 50 inches (127 cm) long. Fold the pieces in half and attach them to the 6-inch (15-cm) ring using a reverse lark's head knot. Attach the cords in between the ⁵⁄₆₄-inch (2-mm) attached cords.

25

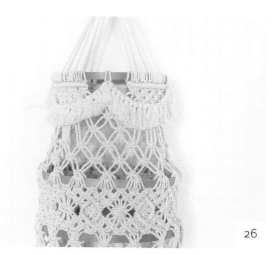

26

27

VARIATION

25. Using ⁵⁄₆₄-inch (2-mm) three-strand rope, cut 1 piece 55½ inches (141 cm) long. Attach it using a continuous reverse lark's head knot to the 8-inch (20-cm) top wood hoop in between each of the 4 sections. Tie the ends together with a reef knot.

26. Using ³⁄₁₆-inch (5-mm) three-strand rope, cut 1 piece 123½ inches (313.6 cm) long. Pull apart the rope so you are left with 3 individual strands. Leaving a 1-inch (2.5-cm) tail, tie a lark's head knot with one of the strands, and cut the other end at 1 inch (2.5 cm) so they are the same length. Do this to each of the 4 sections, filling up the whole section. Unravel the fringe and brush with a large-tooth comb. This is the same technique as steps 11A and B from the Florence Plant Hanger (see photos on pages 106–107 if needed).

27. Cut the ropes from step 22 at 10½ inches (26.5 cm) long and unravel and trim again if desired. On the 6-inch (15-cm) inner ring, unravel the ropes and trim again if desired.

variation

Try leaving out steps 11–20 and tie 3 rows of alternating square knots, leaving the same 1-inch (2.5-cm) gap between each row. Attach the second 10-inch (25.5-cm) embroidery hoop (inside only) the same way you attached the first one in step 10. Continue the steps from 21 onward to complete the lantern. To attach the 6-inch (15-cm) hoop, use 4 pieces of rope cut at 27 inches (68.6 cm), and attach them with a reverse lark's head knot to the second 10-inch (25.4-cm) hoop. Position the 6-inch (15-cm) ring 6 inches (15 cm) below the 10-inch (25.5-cm) ring, and tie 2 double half hitches to secure the hoop in the same 12, 3, 6 and 9 o'clock pattern.

going beyond the projects

I love that macramé truly has endless possibilities of knots, patterns and combinations of the two. This is one of the reasons it can be addicting, and once you fall in love with the craft, your ideas will be endless. In each of the projects in the book you learned a new technique, approach or idea to begin thinking outside the box. I challenge everyone who loves this craft to go beyond these projects and come up with unique and original ideas. I hope some of these concepts will get you excited and bursting with ideas to try!

You can change the look of any project, pattern or design simply by changing the spacing of the knots. Any pattern changes completely when you tie the rows very close together versus leaving space between them. For example, the final look of alternating square knots is completely changed by the amount of spacing between them. Have fun adjusting the spacing between rows and knots to vary designs to your individual style.

You can also change the entire look of a design by using a different diameter rope. The larger the rope, the bulkier a project will look and the larger it will be. By decreasing the size of the rope, your project will look more delicate and possibly even smaller. Remember the Palm Frond Wall Hanging on page 63? This is a perfect example of this concept in action.

Another easy way to change the look of a project is by changing the color of the rope, adding a colored rope, dyeing your rope or even dip dyeing the piece! Remember the Luma Rope Light (page 123)? Adding the black cord created so much contrast within the piece. The neutral tone-on-tone version is subtle in whatever space it's in, whereas the contrast with the added color makes it pop and draws your eye to it.

Another way to alter your macramé pieces is by adding layers to create depth. Remember the Etherea Lantern (page 155) and the Florence Plant Hanger (page 103)? These projects are visually interesting because the layers add depth to the piece. This idea can be applied to almost any type of project.

It's also helpful to think about pairing intricate patterns with simple ones, or playing with negative and positive space. This can also be seen in the Etherea Lantern (page 155) and the Heirloom Table Runner (page 147). In design, positive and negative space is so important, and you can play around with this in macramé by having more or fewer knots. Negative (blank) space is just as important as the knots and patterns (positive space) in your piece because it makes both spaces more impactful.

Reference the knot and pattern section (pages 11 to 39) for additional tips on how to expand beyond each specific pattern and try combining different patterns together in one piece.

I hope you feel inspired to create your own unique macramé pieces using some of these concepts. Don't forget to experiment and try new ideas!

materials source list

Here is a list of places you can buy your rope and other materials.

ROPE AND MATERIAL SUPPLIERS

CANADA
My website: Natalieranae.com
Ropeshop.ca (free Canada-wide shipping on orders over $100)
Etsy.com/ca/shop/BohoMontreal

USA
Modernmacrame.com
Knotandrope.com
Knotstuff.com
Etsy.com/shop/reformfibers
Niromastudio.com
Housesparrownesting.com
Rwrope.com
Bulkropes.com

AUSTRALIA
Marymakerstudio.com.au
Edeneve.com.au
Familythreds.com

NEW ZEALAND
Etsy.com/shop/knottybloom

EUROPE
Teddyandwool.etsy.com
Createaholic.tictail.com
Etsy.com/shop/miniswells

PORTUGAL
c-a-s-u-l-o.com

METAL HOOPS
Michaels.com
Joann.com
Createforless.com
Modernmacrame.com
Etsy.com/shop/AllTheMemories
Darice.com

LARGE-EYE NEEDLES
Michaels.com
Joann.com
Createforless.com
Fabricland.com
Amazon.com

WOODEN BEADS
Etsy.com/shop/TheBeadedBead
Modernmacrame.com

MISCELLANEOUS

MILK CRATES
Amazon.com: Milk crates are great for conveniently cutting rope (see page 41)—I often also find used ones being recycled or at curbs

SHEARS
Amazon.com
Wisstool.com: Wiss 2DAN 7¾-inch (20-cm) leverage shears

LIGHTING
Amazon.com
Globe-electric.com: Plug-in socket pendant lights

IKEA
"Rigga" clothing rack
"Grundtal" pack of 5 large metal S-hooks
"Sekond" light cord set

acknowledgments

I wouldn't be able to even begin thanking people if I didn't start with my incredible husband, who was by my side supporting me throughout this entire process. He truly is the embodiment of a loving, caring and supportive husband and I don't know how I'll ever thank him for all he's done and sacrificed for me while I was writing this book. Thank you to my encouraging and loving family, who were with me every step of the way and continuously prayed for me. Thank you to my friends, who gave me grace and understanding while I was focused on writing this book. Thank you, Jenn, for all your hard work, carving out time for me and bringing my vision to life through your beautiful photography. A huge thank-you to Page Street for giving me this opportunity and believing in me. And most importantly, thank you, God, for this opportunity and for being with me through this entire journey. As an artist and maker, I find all of my inspiration through You, the original Creator and Artist.

about the author

Natalie Ranae is a self-taught macramé artist who made her first plant hanger and didn't look back. She fell in love with the craft and made a career from it, teaching workshops all over Ontario, selling original designs on her website and creating large-scale custom orders for clients. She splits her time working out of her home studio surrounded by her three cats and a co-working studio for creatives that she co-founded with her best friend Jenn, called Kindred Loft. Graduating from OCAD University with a bachelor's degree in design, Natalie majored in and is also a professional jeweler and metalsmith. She has never limited herself to one form of creating and loves goldsmithing, knitting, crocheting, woodworking and whatever else she decides she wants to learn. Her unique approach to design and her attention to detail are consistent across any medium she works in. When she isn't making or working on growing her business, Natalie spends her time tackling DIYs with her husband on their 100-year-old house, volunteering locally and watering the jungle of plants in her home. Who says you can't be a crazy cat and plant lady?!

You can find Natalie on Instagram at @natalie_ranae and on her website natalieranae.com. Tag her in your finished and in-process projects on Instagram!

index